Ruth
Elijah
Jonah

Pre-K & K, Summer
Teacher Guide

Group

Loveland, Colorado

www.HandsOnBible.com

Group's R.E.A.L. Guarantee

Every Group resource incorporates "R.E.A.L. Learning"—a unique approach that results in long-term retention and life transformation. It's learning that's:

R = Relational
Learner-to-learner talk involves everyone, enhances understanding, and builds Christian friendships.

E = Experiential
Learning by doing and using multiple senses increases learning and retention up to tenfold.

A = Applicable
Connecting God's Word to the learners' real world moves learning beyond information to transformation.

L = Learner-Based
Addressing how learners learn best focuses not on how much is taught, but on what is learned.

Group®

Hands-On Bible Curriculum™, Pre-K & K, Summer
Copyright © 1995 Group Publishing, Inc.

2001 edition

Visit our Web site: **www.grouppublishing.com**

Credits
Contributing Authors: Melissa C. Downey, Nanette Goings, and Liz Shockey
Editors: Susan L. Lingo and Jan Kershner
Senior Editor: Lois Keffer
Chief Creative Officer: Joani Schultz
Copy Editor: Pamela Shoup
Art Director: Helen Lannis
Cover Art Directors: Debbie Collins and DeWain Stoll
Cover Designer: DeWain Stoll
Designers: Lisa Chandler and Jean Bruns
Computer Graphic Artist: Randy Kady
Cover Photographer: Bohm-Marrazzo
Illustrators: Jan Knudson, Judy Love, and Bonnie Matthews
Audio Engineer: Steve Saavedra
Production Manager: Dodie Tipton

ISBN 0-7644-0243-9
Printed in the United States of America.
10 9 8 7 6 5 4 3 2 1   03 02 01

section lets them jump up and wear out the wiggles without wiggling away from the lesson!

Practicing The Point

● **Practicing The Point lets children practice and teach what they've learned.** In this section, children interact with a puppet friend about The Point. You can use Pockets the Kangaroo, available from Group Publishing, or any puppet of your choice. You can even make your own kangaroo puppet. Pockets is energetic and friendly. She truly wants to understand The Point, but often needs to have it explained a few times before she gets it right.

You'll be amazed to discover how much your children have learned as they share the lesson with Pockets. Even children who are shy around adults will open up to Pockets. After several weeks, children will begin to expect Pockets' regular visits and will be eager to set her straight.

For a change of pace, try one of the following ideas for bringing Pockets into other parts of the lesson:
● Have Pockets greet children as they arrive.
● Have children tell the Bible story to Pockets.
● Have Pockets participate in games or other activities.
● Have Pockets ask questions to draw out shy children.
● Have Pockets give the attention-getting signal.
● Have Pockets encourage disruptive children to quiet down.
● Use Pockets to snuggle or hug children.

You can purchase Pockets in your local Christian bookstore or directly from Group Publishing by calling 1-800-447-1070.

Closing

● **The closing activity gives you an opportunity to repeat The Point once more and wrap up the class session.** As you complete the closing activity, encourage children to say The Point with you. Encourage them to share The Point with their families when they go home.

For Extra Time

● **If you have a long class period, or simply want to add variety to your lessons, try one of the For Extra Time activities.** For Extra Time activities include learning games, crafts, and snacks related to the lesson, as well as suggestions to enhance each lesson's story picture. Most of these ideas could also be used in the Let's Get Started section of the lesson. Each For Extra Time activity lists the supplies you'll need.

Today I Learned...

● **The photocopiable "Today I Learned..." handout helps parents and children interact about the lesson.** Each handout includes a verse to learn, family activity ideas, a story picture, and an "Ask Me..." section with questions for parents to ask their children about the lesson. Encourage parents to use the handout to help them reinforce what their children are learning at church.

Understanding Your 5- and 6-Year-Olds

Physical Development

- Developing fine motor skills.
- Most can use scissors and color within the lines.
- Developing hand-eye coordination; can copy patterns, handle paste or glue, and tie shoes.

Emotional Development

- Proud of their accomplishments.
- Have their feelings hurt easily.
- Beginning to gain self-confidence.

Social Development

- Learning to share and cooperate.
- Can understand and follow rules.
- Enjoy extensive dramatic play.
- Eager to please teachers and parents.

Mental Development

- Can listen to and create stories.
- Can distinguish between real and pretend.
- Need simple directions—understand one step at a time.

Spiritual Development

- Understand that God made them.
- Trust that God loves them.
- Beginning to develop sense of conscience.

Dear Parent,

I'm so glad to be your child's teacher this quarter. With our Hands-On Bible Curriculum™, your child will look at the Bible in a whole new way.

For the next 13 weeks, 5- and 6-year-olds will learn about such memorable Bible characters as Ruth, Elijah, and Jonah and how they obeyed God. Using active- and interactive-learning methods and exciting storytelling tools such as Group's Bible Big Books™ and Group's Learning Mat™, we'll help children discover, understand, and apply God's Word.

Our Hands-On Bible Curriculum welcomes you to play an important part in what your child learns. **Each week when you pick up your child, you'll receive a "Today I Learned . . ." handout.** "Today I Learned . . ." tells you what we did in class and provides you with questions and activities to help you reinforce your child's Bible lesson at home.

Let me encourage you to use the "Today I Learned . . ." handout regularly; it's a great tool for reinforcing Bible truths and promoting positive, healthy communication in your family.

Sincerely,

Ruth

Families help each other. In good times and hard times, the love family members share for each other is a reflection of God's unchanging love. The story of Ruth beautifully exemplifies these values. Ruth's commitment to Naomi and obedience to Naomi's motherly direction bring a happy ending to a story begun in sorrow.

The 5- and 6-year-olds in your class are beginning to define their places in the world by learning their roles in the family. Sharing doesn't always come naturally, and jealousy is likely to crop up from time to time. But by learning God's plan for families, they begin to see how to behave in the world. Through the following lessons, children will realize that God made families, and God wants families to love and help each other.

Four Lessons on the Story of Ruth

	Page	Point	Bible Basis
Lesson 1 **Family Friends**	17	Families help each other.	Ruth 1:1-18
Lesson 2 **Hard-Time Help**	31	Families help each other in hard times.	Ruth 1:19–2:3
Lesson 3 **Families Share**	43	Families help each other and share with each other.	Ruth 2:4-23
Lesson 4 **Families Celebrate**	55	Families help each other and celebrate together.	Ruth 3:1–4:16

Time Stretchers

Harvest Freeze Tag

Use tape to mark lines on the floor dividing the room into two sections, one larger than the other. The smaller section is the safety zone. The larger section is the grainfield. Have children form pairs. One pair will be the Harvest Family. They'll stand in the grainfield to protect it. The other pairs will go to the safety zone. Direct pairs to lock arms. The object of the game is for the pairs in the safety zone to cross the grainfield, touch the wall, and return to the safety zone without being tagged by the Harvest Family. Tell the Harvest Family to shuffle their feet during this game—their feet can't leave the floor. All other pairs must walk heel-to-toe during the game. Pairs who get tagged must freeze. Continue playing until only one pair remains. This pair will become the Harvest Family for the next game.

Winnowing We'll Go

Explain to the children that in Bible times, harvesting grain involved reaping, threshing, and winnowing. Winnowing meant separating the grain from the chaff or stalks by tossing the grain in the air onto a round screen.

Make two or three winnowing screens by pulling a coat hanger into an oval shape. Stretch a pantyhose leg over the oval and wrap tape around the hose at the handle. You may want to let children help make the screens. Form an assembly line with three groups—one to hold the ovals, one to stretch the pantyhose, and one to tape.

Give each group of children a finished screen and two large dried lima beans. Have the children take turns tossing the beans in the air and catching them again on the screen five times, much like harvesters did to winnow the grain.

I Can Help Song

Teach children this fun action song to the tune of "Did You Ever See a Lassie." (Note: this song is not recorded on the *CD*.)

I can help my family, my family, my family (*point to self*);
I can help my family by lending a hand. (*Extend hand.*)
I'll help with the dishes (*pretend to dry dishes*)
And help where Mom wishes.
I can help my family by lending a hand. (*Extend hand.*)

I can help my brother, and sister, and cousin (*point to others*);
I can help my family by sharing my toys.
I'll share my wagon (*pretend to pull a wagon*),
My skates and stuffed dragon. (*Pretend to hug a stuffed animal.*)
I can help my family by sharing my toys.

I can help God's family, God's family, God's family;
I can help God's family by doing what's right. (*Nod head yes.*)
I'll help and I'll share (*hold hands out*),
And I'll show that I care. (*Hand to heart.*)
I can help God's family by doing what's right! (*Nod head yes.*)

Remembering God's Word

Each four- or five-week module focuses on a key Bible verse. The key verse for this module is "As for me and my household, we will serve the Lord" (Joshua 24:15b).

This module's key verse will teach children that God is pleased when we love and care for our families. Have fun using these ideas anytime during the lessons on families.

Family Blocks

Give each child a paper plate or a sheet of paper. Ask each child to draw a picture of a family member on the plate. You may want to form groups and have one group draw moms, another group draw dads, and a third group draw siblings or grandparents.

Tape a line on the floor and place plates on the floor behind it. Give each child a wrapped hard candy to use as a game piece. Have children take turns stepping up to the line and tossing the candy onto one of the plates. When the candy lands on a plate, ask the child to describe a way the person pictured on the plate could help his or her family. For example, a grandmother could bake cookies or baby-sit, a child could set the table for dinner, and a parent could buy groceries. After all children have taken their turns, they may unwrap and eat their candy game pieces.

Welcome Mat

Tell the children you're going to play a game similar to musical chairs called the Welcome Mat game. Have as many sheets of construction paper as there are children in your class. Draw a smile on half of the papers. Tape all the papers in a circle on the floor. Be sure that the smiles are facing up. The children will hop from paper to paper, singing the following song to the tune of "Here We Go 'Round the Mulberry Bush." (Note: this song is not recorded on the *CD*.)

> **As for me and my household, household, household,**
> **As for me and my household,**
> **We will serve the Lord.**

As you hop around the circle, sing the song through a few times until children are familiar with the words. Tell them that the next time you sing it, you'll all stop hopping when the song ends. The children standing on the smiles when the song ends will get to repeat the Bible verse. Repeat the song three or four times.

Story Enhancements

Make Bible stories come alive in your classroom by bringing in Bible costumes, setting out sensory items that fit with the story, or creating an exciting bulletin board to stimulate interest. The following ideas will help you get started.

Lesson 1

● Create interest in each week's lesson by placing a table near the entry door of your classroom. Each week add a new item(s) to the table. For this lesson, bring in leather sandals. Let children try them on and carefully walk around the room in them. Explain that in Bible times, people had to walk everywhere, and they wore sandals as they walked. Talk about how people travel today. You may want to bring in model cars, planes, or trains to place on the table with the sandals to illustrate how times have changed.

Ask children what it would be like to walk everywhere today. Tell them that today's Bible story is about a family who walked a long way together.

● Bring in scarves and headbands for children to use for dress up. Tell children the people in today's Bible story wore scarves to protect them from the heat and wind while they worked in the fields.

Lesson 2

● For this week's lesson, bring in a variety of cereals to taste. These may include puffed rice, oatmeal, corn flakes, wheat germ, and shredded wheat. Talk about how grains are ground and used for many foods.

● Let children plant seeds of your choice in small plastic containers or peat pots. Talk about how people in Bible times had to rely on what they planted for food—they couldn't just go to the grocery store.

Lesson 3

● For this week's lesson, add a bushelbasket next to the table. Put a bowl of popcorn inside it. Explain that in Ruth's time, people had to pick up enough grain to fill a bushelbasket many times. They had to gather enough for whole year! Let each child take a few pieces of popcorn as a quick snack.

● Bring in farm or garden tools such as a shovel, rake, and hand trowel for children to see and carefully touch.

● Ask someone in your church who is an avid gardener to talk to your class. Have the gardener talk about the work that goes into a garden and bring in something he or she has grown.

Lesson 4

● This week, add a bowl of flowers or flower petals. (Note: craft stores often sell discounted silk flowers that have become detached from stems.) Explain that people use flowers in lots of ways at weddings—for bouquets, decorations, and to scatter on the ground in front of the bride. Let children strew flowers in a pretend wedding procession.

● Bring in small musical instruments such as harmonicas, kazoos, and a small electronic keyboard. Explain how music was a big part of most celebrations in Ruth's time. Talk about how people in Bible times used music to praise God. Let children try out the instruments.

● Bring in wedding photos and pictures of family celebrations. Let children go through the pictures and talk about what's happening in each one. Explain how weddings and parties in Bible times often lasted a whole week!

Family Friends

The Bible Basis

Ruth 1:1-18. Ruth wants to stay with Naomi and return to Bethlehem with her.

Not enough to eat. A family to feed. Facing these problems, Elimelech and Naomi moved their family from Bethlehem to Moab, where there was more food. After Elimelech's death, Naomi raised their sons, who grew up and married Moabite women, Orpah and Ruth. After her sons died, a disheartened Naomi wanted to return to Bethlehem. Ruth and Orpah said they'd return with her, but Naomi told them to stay. So Orpah stayed in Moab; Ruth insisted on returning to Bethlehem with Naomi. Ruth made a wise choice—a choice that begins the story of how a Gentile woman became the great-grandmother of King David and an ancestor of the King of Kings, Jesus.

Five- and 6-year-olds need the security of a loving family. After a long day at school or a squabble with a friend, they need the support and encouragement their families can offer. As children learn about family loyalty in this lesson, they'll begin to see that the commitment in their own families is no accident, but part of God's loving plan. Use this lesson to teach that God wants families to help each other.

Getting the Point

✏ **Families help each other.**

It's important to say The Point just as it's written in each activity. Repeating The Point over and over will help the children remember it and apply it to their lives.

Children will
● hear how Ruth helped her family,
● share ways they can help their own families,
● help Pockets understand family relationships, and
● discover that families are important to God.

✏ **The Point**

This Lesson at a Glance

Before the lesson, collect the necessary items for the activities you plan to use. Refer to the Classroom Supplies and Learning Lab Supplies columns to determine what you'll need. Remember to make photocopies of the "Today I Learned..." handout (p. 30) to send home with your children.

Section	Minutes	What Children Will Do	Classroom Supplies	Learning Lab Supplies
Welcome Time	up to 5	**Welcome!**—Receive name tags and be greeted by the teacher.	"Family Name Tags" handouts (p. 29), markers, tape or pins	
Let's Get Started Direct children to one or more of the Let's Get Started activities until everyone arrives.	up to 10	**Option 1: Family Bracelets**—Make colorful bead bracelets to tell about their families.	Elastic thread; red, white, yellow, and blue beads; scissors; muffin cups	
	up to 10	**Option 2: Family Tree**—Make a family tree to help tell the Bible story.	"Story Faces" handout (p. 28), brown paper grocery sacks, yellow and green construction paper, tape, scissors, marker	
	up to 10	**Option 3: Journey Blocks**—Lay a pretend road and travel from Bethlehem to Moab.	Building blocks	
Pick-Up Song	up to 5	**We Will Pick Up**—Sing a song as they pick up toys and gather for the Bible story.	CD player	CD: "We Will Pick Up" (track 2)
Bible-Story Time	up to 5	**Setting the Stage**—Play an unusual game and learn how families stay close.	Paper cups, toothpick, markers, string, scissors, aluminum foil	
	up to 5	**Bible Song and Prayer Time**—Sing a song, bring out the Bible, and pray together.	Bible, construction paper, scissors, basket or box, CD player	CD: "God's Book" (track 3), family stamp and ink pad
	up to 10	**Hear the Bible Story**—Use the family tree to tell how Ruth stayed with Naomi (from Ruth 1:1-18).	Bible, family tree from Option 2, green construction paper	Bible Big Book: Ruth (p. 1)
	up to 10	**Do the Bible Story**—Play a fun game and learn how families help each other.		Family stamp and ink pad
Practicing the Point	up to 5	**Helping Hands**—Teach Pockets that families help each other.	Pockets the Kangaroo, kerchief, feather duster	
Closing	up to 5	**I Can Help**—Tell one way to help their families and sing a song.	CD player, Come-Back Cups from "Setting the Stage"	CD: "God Made Families" (track 4)
For Extra Time	For extra-time ideas and supplies, see page 27.			

Families help each other.

Welcome Time

Welcome! (up to 5 minutes)

- Bend down to make eye contact with children as they arrive.
- Greet each child individually with an enthusiastic smile.
- Thank each child for coming to class today.
- Say: **Today we're going to learn that ✏ families help each other.**
- Give each child a photocopy of a name tag from the "Family Name Tag" handout (p. 29). Help children write their names on their name tags and pin or tape them to their clothing. You may want to cover the name tags in clear adhesive paper so that name tags will last for the entire module.
- Direct the children to the Let's Get Started activities you've set up.

✏ **The Point**

Let's Get Started

Set up one or more of the following activities for children to do as they arrive. After you greet each child, invite him or her to choose an activity.

Circulate among children to guide the activities and direct children's conversation toward today's lesson. Ask questions such as "How do families help each other?" or "How can families show God their love?"

OPTION 1: Family Bracelets (up to 10 minutes)

Before class, cut a 7-inch length of elastic thread for each child. Tie a double knot at the end of each thread.

Set out muffin cups containing white, red, blue, or yellow beads, separated by color. As children arrive, invite them to make bracelets that tell about their family members. Use red beads to represent fathers, white beads for mothers, blue beads for themselves, and yellow beads for brothers and sisters. Tell children they may also choose a color to represent a family pet. Children may string as many beads of each color as they choose.

As children string their beads, encourage them to tell about family members. Ask questions such as "What's one special thing your family does together?" and "Why do you think God made families?" Point out that God made families so that ✏ families help each other. Tell children they'll hear a Bible story about a woman named Ruth and how people in her family helped each other.

✏ **The Point**

When the beads are strung, help children tie the ends of their threads together to form bracelets. Let them wear their bracelets to show how glad they are that God made families.

✔ Many children live in families impacted by divorce. Be sensitive to the fact that children in your class may come from single-parent and step-family situations. Encourage children by sharing how God loves their families and takes care of them, even when they're not together.

OPTION 2: Family Tree (up to 10 minutes)

Before class cut four paper grocery sacks so you can flatten them out. Cut two of the sacks in thirds. Photocopy the "Story Faces" handout on page 28. Cut out the pictures of the characters' faces. Set aside Boaz's picture until next week.

Set out tape, grocery sacks, story pictures, and green and yellow construction paper. Let children construct a cooperative family tree on a bulletin board or wall. Form three groups: Trunk Twisters, Branch Builders, and Leaf Layers. Trunk Twisters twist the two whole sacks into a trunk and tape it to the bulletin board. Branch Builders twist and bend the pieces of sack into tree branches. Then have them tape the branches to the trunk. Leaf Layers tear green construction paper leaves and tape a Story Face to each leaf. Set aside a leaf to use with the picture of Boaz next week. Let everyone work together to tape the leaves on the tree. Tell children to tear one yellow leaf and tape it to the treetop. Write the word "God" on the yellow leaf.

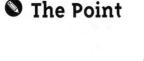 **The Point**

As children work together, make comments such as "Did you know that families are really important to God?" and "I like the way you're helping each other with this tree." Explain that ◗ families help each other, and today's Bible story is about a family who stayed together and helped each other.

> ✔ The way the characters in the story of Ruth are related to each other can be confusing for young children. Be sure to make a family tree either as an Option or before the module. The family tree will clarify how the characters are related to each other.

OPTION 3: Journey Blocks (up to 10 minutes)

Set building blocks in one corner of the room. As children arrive, let them build a long, winding road with blocks. Then have them walk beside the blocks and follow the road to the end and back again. Ask children where their pretend road leads. Tell children that today they'll hear a Bible story about a family who walked all the way from Bethlehem to the land of Moab—about 50 miles. And later, two of the family members traveled all the way back. Ask questions such as "Has your family ever moved? What was that like?" and "How do families help each other get ready to move or go on trips?" Point out that God made families and that ◗ families help each other. Have children build other roads to follow.

The Point

When everyone has arrived and you're ready to move on to the Bible-Story Time, encourage the children to finish what they're doing and get ready to clean up.

Pick-Up Song

We Will Pick Up (up to 5 minutes)

Lead children in singing "We Will Pick Up" (track 2) with the *CD* to the tune of "London Bridge." Encourage the children to sing along as they help clean up the room.

You'll be using this song each week to alert children to start picking up. At first, they may need a little encouragement. But after a few weeks, picking up and singing along will become a familiar routine.

If you want to include the names of all the children in your class, sing the song without the *CD* and repeat the naming section. If you choose to use the *CD,* vary the names you use each week.

Sing

We will pick up all our toys,
All our toys, all our toys.
We will pick up all our toys
And put them all away.

I see (name) picking up
Picking up, picking up.
I see (name) picking up
And putting toys away.

(Repeat.)

Bible-Story Time

Setting the Stage (up to 5 minutes)

Tell the children you'll clap your hands to get their attention. Explain that when you clap your hands, children are to stop what they're doing, raise their hands, and focus on you. Encourage children to respond quickly so you'll have time for all the fun activities you've planned.

Before class, use a toothpick to poke a hole through the bottom of a paper cup. Thread a 10-inch string down through the hole and tie a knot to keep the string from pulling completely through the cup. Prepare one cup for each child.

Gather children in a circle. Set markers and 6-inch squares of aluminum foil in the center. Hand each child a paper cup. Say: **We're going to make Come-Back Cups. Use markers to decorate your cups. Then crumple a piece of aluminum foil around the end of the string.**

When children are finished making their cups, say: **Hold your cup and swing the foil ball in the air. See if you can catch the ball in your cup.** Allow children to play with their Come-Back Cups. For extra fun, have them count the number of catches in a 15-second period. Then ask:

● **What happened each time you swung the ball?** (It went in the air; it came down; it came back to the cup.)

● **How did you catch the ball?** (I moved the cup; I aimed it.)

Say: **Just as you helped the foil ball return to your cup, families help each other stay together. If family members go to school or jobs or the store, they come back. God made families and he wants them to stay** close and help each other. You can think of your cup as your family, and the foil ball as you. The string is the love you feel for your family and that's what keeps you coming back! Let's swing our foil balls and catch them again. Pause for children to respond.

Say: **Let's hear a Bible story about a family who stayed together and helped each other. The story will help us remember that ⬤ families help each other.** Have children set their Come-Back Cups against a wall.

● The Point

Bible Song and Prayer Time (up to 5 minutes)

Before class, make surprise cards for this activity by cutting construction paper into 2×6-inch slips. Prepare a surprise card for each child plus a few extras for visitors. Fold the cards in half, then stamp the *family stamp* inside one of the surprise cards. Mark Ruth 1:1-18 in the Bible you'll be using.

TEACHER TIPS

✔ Choose a Bible you'll use for this section of the lesson each week. A children's Bible or an easy-to-understand translation works best. Some of the children in your class may be reading. If children can understand the words in the Bible, they'll have more interest in reading it—and they'll learn more from it.

Note:
If the ink pad is dry, moisten it with three to five drops of water.

Have children sit in a circle. Say: **Now it's time to choose a Bible person to bring me the Bible marked with today's Bible story. Before I choose today's Bible person, let's learn our Bible song. As we sing, I'll pass out surprise cards. Don't look inside your surprise card until the song is over.**

Lead children in singing "God's Book" (track 3) with the *CD* to the tune of "Old MacDonald Had a Farm." As you sing, pass out the folded surprise cards. If you want to include the names of all the children in your class, sing the song without the *CD* and repeat the naming section. If you choose to use the *CD*, vary the names you use each week.

Sing 🎵

Now it's time to read God's Book
And hear a Bible story.
It's fun to be here with my
     friends
And hear a Bible story.

(Name)'s here,
(Name)'s here.
Here is (name).
Here is (name).
Now it's time to read God's Book
And hear a Bible story.

Now it's time to read God's Book
And hear a Bible story.
It's fun to be here with my
     friends
And hear a Bible story.

(Name)'s here.
(Name)'s here.
Here is (name).
Here is (name).
Now it's time to read God's Book
And hear a Bible story.

After the song, say: **You may look inside your surprise cards. The person who has the family stamped inside his or her card will be our Bible person for today.**

Families help each other.

Identify the Bible person, then have the rest of the children clap for him or her. Ask the Bible person to bring you the Bible. Help the Bible person open the Bible to the marked place and show the children where your story comes from. Then have the Bible person sit down.

Say: (Name) **was our special Bible person today. Each week we'll have only one Bible person, but each one of you is a special part of our class! Today we're all learning that** **families help each other.**

Let's say a special prayer now and ask God to teach us to help our families. I'll pass around this basket. When the basket comes to you, put your surprise card in it and say, "God, please teach me to help my family."

Pass around the basket or box. When you've collected everyone's surprise card, set the basket aside and pick up the Bible.

> ✔ You'll probably be able to reuse most of the surprise cards from last week. Throw out any torn or crumpled cards and make enough new ones for each child to have one. Keep a list of who's had the surprise card to ensure that everyone gets a turn to be the Bible person.

Lead the children in this prayer: **God, thank you for the Bible and all the stories in it. Teach us today that** **families help each other. In Jesus' name we pray, amen.**

Hear the Bible Story (up to 10 minutes)

Before this activity, tear a green construction paper leaf for each child. Be sure you've taped the leaves with the story faces to the family tree you made in Option 2. Set the leaf with the picture of Boaz aside for next week.

Gather children in front of the family tree for the Bible story. Hold up the Bible. Say: **Our story today comes from the book of Ruth in the Bible.** Hold up the *Bible Big Book: Ruth.* Say: **Our Big Book shows us pictures of the story. Before we begin, let's look at the family tree on the bulletin board. The family tree will help us learn about the people in our story.** Point to the yellow leaf on the treetop. **This leaf is for God. He's on top of the tree because God is our heavenly Father. He made families, and all families come from God.**

Point to the leaves with the pictures of Elimelech and Naomi. Say: **This is Elimelech** (Eh-LIM-eh-leck) **and Naomi** (Nay-OH-me). **Let's say those names together. Elimelech. Naomi. Elimelech and Naomi were husband and wife. They had two sons.** Point to their pictures. **The sons each married. One married a girl named Orpah** (OR-puh). Point to Orpah. **Let's say her name together. Orpah. The other married a girl named Ruth.** Point to Ruth's picture.

Say: **Look at all the people on the tree. And they were all in the same family! Let's see if you can remember where their pictures are. I'll say one of the names. If you know where his or her picture is, put your hand on your head. Then I'll have someone point to the leaf with that story picture.** Call the following story names and choose one or two children to point out each picture: Elimelech, Naomi, the two sons, Orpah, Ruth, and God.

Say: **You did a great job remembering the story people. Now let's hear the Bible story. You can help me, but first you need special leaves.** Hand each child a green construction paper leaf. **When I say the name of someone whose picture is on the family tree, raise your arms like tree branches and wave your leaves.**

Open the Big Book to page 1. Read the following story, pausing at each underlined name.

Long ago in the land of Judah, people went hungry because there wasn't enough food. <u>Elimelech,</u> his wife <u>Naomi,</u> and their <u>two sons</u> moved to the country of Moab, where there was plenty of food for everyone.

Then a sad thing happened. <u>Elimelech</u> died. But <u>Naomi</u> still had her <u>two sons.</u> They grew up and married women named <u>Orpah</u> and <u>Ruth.</u> But then <u>Naomi's</u> sons died, too. <u>Naomi</u> and her daughters-in-law were left all alone. How sad!

<u>Naomi</u> decided to go back to her own country. So she packed her things and started off to Bethlehem. <u>Ruth</u> and <u>Orpah</u> said, "We'll go with you." <u>Naomi</u> shook her head. "Your mothers live here and I have no way to care for you. Stay here with your families in Moab." So <u>Orpah</u> decided to stay.

But <u>Ruth</u> loved <u>Naomi</u> and couldn't say goodbye. "Where you go, I will go. I want to live with your family and serve your God," she insisted. So <u>Ruth</u> and <u>Naomi</u> started off on the long trip to Bethlehem together.

Close the Big Book. Ask:
● **Why did Elimelech help his family by moving them to Moab?** (To find more food; there wasn't enough to eat.)
● **How did the family in the story stay together?** (They moved together; they decided to go back to Bethlehem together; they helped each other.)
● **Why do you think Ruth stayed with Naomi?** (Ruth loved Naomi; they were in the same family.)

Say: **Even though it meant leaving her homeland, Ruth stayed with Naomi. Naomi loved Ruth like her own daughter. Ruth loved Naomi like a real mother, even though Naomi was her mother-in-law. And Naomi helped Ruth learn about God.**
● **How did Ruth help Naomi?** (By staying with her; by going back to Bethlehem with her; by loving Naomi.)

Say: **Ruth knew that a wonderful mother-in-law like Naomi was a gift from God. Ruth also knew that ◉ families help each other, so she wanted to help her mother-in-law. Let's play a game to show how families can help each other—and have fun!**

Return the Big Book to the Learning Lab. Save the story-picture leaves to use with later lessons.

Do the Bible Story (up to 10 minutes)

● **The Point**

Set the *family stamp and ink pad* on a chair to one side of the room. Say: **Today we're learning how families stay together and how ◉ families help each other. Let's play a game and pretend our family is going to Moab. I'll choose a family leader. He or she can tag others to join the family. If you're tagged, go to the chair and stamp your hand. Then help tag others.**

Families help each other.

Play until all children have been tagged and have had their hands stamped. If time permits, play the game again without the stamp.

When the game is finished, say: **That was fun! You stayed together and helped each other until everyone was tagged. Just as Ruth and Naomi stayed together and helped each other, our families can, too.** Ask:

● **Can you think of a time when families help each other?** (When someone is sick; when you move.)

Say: **That's right. Families love each other, so**  **families help each other. I wonder if our friend Pockets knows how to help her family.**

● **The Point**

Practicing the Point

Helping Hands (up to 5 minutes)

Before class, tie a kerchief around Pockets' neck or head, and have a feather duster or cleaning brush sticking out of her pocket. Have children sit in a circle. Take out Pockets the Kangaroo and go through the following script. When you finish the script, put Pockets out of sight.

Helping Hands

PUPPET SCRIPT

Pockets: *(Wiping her forehead)* Whew, am I tired!

Teacher: Hi, Pockets! What have you been doing?

Pockets: I've just been cleaning my room, and it was hard work. Mom asked me to help around the house 'cause we're having company.

Teacher: Why, Pockets. That was very nice of you. You must feel good about helping.

Pockets: Not really! I thought I would get a quarter for helping, but I didn't get anything!

Teacher: You don't have to get money to help, do you?

Pockets: Yes! Yesterday Dad gave me a quarter for helping wash the car, so I figured I'd get a quarter for cleaning my room, too. That's the only reason I did it!

Teacher: Now Pockets, I bet that's not the only reason you helped. Families help each other because families love each other. Children, let's tell Pockets about our Bible story and how Ruth helped her family. *(Encourage children to tell Pockets that Ruth didn't have to help—she helped because she loved Naomi.)*

Pockets: I helped my family 'cause I wanted a quarter.

Teacher: And why else?

Pockets: Well, I love my family... and I do like to help them... and

(Continued)

● **The Point**

Families help each other.

Lesson 1 ● 25

The Point

that's more important than a quarter, right?

Teacher: Right. You're part of a family, and families help each other.

Pockets: Thanks for helping me understand. I think I'll go home and see if my family needs any more help. 'Bye, everyone!

(Have children say goodbye to Pockets.)

TODAY I LEARNED . . .

We believe that Christian education extends beyond the classroom into the home. Photocopy the "Today I Learned . . ." handout (p. 30) for this week and send it home with your children. Encourage parents to use the handout to plan meaningful family activities to reinforce this week's topic. Follow up the "Today I Learned . . ." activities next week by asking children what their families did.

Closing

I Can Help (up to 5 minutes)

The Point

Form pairs or trios. Hand children their Come-Back Cups. Say: **We've been learning that 🖊 families help each other. Let's use our cups to help us look for ways to help our families this week. When I flip the lights, toss your foil ball in the air and catch it in your cup. When you catch it, tell your group one way you can help your family this week, such as setting the table or picking up your toys.**

The Point

Flip the lights a few times to be sure everyone has a turn. Then say: **Let's join hands in our groups and pray together.** Pray: **Dear God, thank you for our families. Help us remember that 🖊 families help each other. In Jesus' name, amen.**

Say: **Before you go, let's sing a song about how God made families.**

Lead children in singing "God Made Families" (track 4) to the tune of "Frère Jacques" with the *CD*. Let children toss and catch the foil balls with their Come-Back Cups as you sing.

Sing 🎵

God made families.
God made families.
To show his love.
To show his love.
We can stick together.
We can help each other.
And show God's love.
And show God's love.

Families help each other.

For Extra Time

If you have a long class time or want to add additional elements to your lesson, try one of the following activities.

LIVELY LEARNING: Work Together

Form family groups of three. Have children in each group stand side by side, locking arms. Give each "family" a pencil. Using only their feet, have groups roll their pencils to the other side of the room and back.

After all families have completed the game, talk about how they had to work together and help each other to move the pencil. Remind children that ⬤ families help each other.

⬤ **The Point**

MAKE TO TAKE: Building God's Family

Give children blown-up balloons and ask them to draw pictures of their families on the balloons with markers. When they've finished, ask them to form pairs and rub balloons on each other's hair to create static electricity. Quickly have them stick balloons to the same wall, forming a group representing God's family. Remind children that just as the balloons stick to the wall, ⬤ families help each other and stick together.

⬤ **The Point**

TREAT TO EAT: Walking Snack

When making the long walk to Bethlehem, Ruth and Naomi probably ate foods such as bread, hard cheese, and dried fruit.

Give each child a paper towel, two or three cheese cubes, a cracker, and an apple slice to fold in the paper towel. If it's a nice day, take a walk outside, eating the snacks as you go. As children walk and eat, ask what they think Ruth and Naomi talked about on the trip to Bethlehem. Remind children that Ruth went with Naomi because ⬤ families help each other.

> **Note:**
> Before preparing the snacks, make sure children are not allergic to the ingredients.

⬤ **The Point**

STORY PICTURE: Ruth Goes With Naomi

Hand each child a photocopy of the "Today I Learned..." handout from page 30. Set out scissors, glue sticks, and small scraps of colorful cloth. Have children glue scraps of cloth to the shawls on the picture of Ruth and Naomi. As they work, talk about ways Ruth and Naomi helped each other in the Bible story. Remind them that ⬤ families help each other.

⬤ **The Point**

Story Faces

Photocopy this page. Cut out the story faces.

Families help each other.

Family Name Tags

Photocopy this page. Cut out the name tags.

Families help each other.

TODAY I LEARNED...

The Point ✏ Families help each other.

Today your child learned that families help each other. Children learned that Ruth helped her mother-in-law, Naomi. They talked about ways they can help their own families.

Verse to Learn

"As for me and my household, we will serve the Lord" (Joshua 24:15b).

Ask Me...

● Why did Ruth choose to go with Naomi?
● How can I help my family?
● How can our family show we love God?

Family Fun

● Make a family-memory scrapbook from old photographs and pictures drawn by the children to recount favorite trips, adventures, or special events shared by the family.
● Enjoy a family "stick together" snack, using peanut butter or marshmallow creme between graham crackers. As you make your snacks, talk about ways you've stuck together as a family.

Ruth Goes With Naomi (Ruth 1:1-18)

Hard-Time Help

LESSON 2

The Bible Basis

Ruth 1:19–2:3. Ruth gathers grain in the fields.

Naomi and Ruth arrived in Bethlehem, but the homecoming brought hardship. Even obtaining food posed a problem. Because Naomi was too old to work in the fields, Ruth set out to gather grain alone. By law (Deuteronomy 24:19-22), the poor could gather what little the reapers in the fields left behind. For Ruth, the task was probably threatening. A Moabite girl could expect abuse from the Judean workers (Numbers 25). Yet her love for Naomi gave Ruth the courage to face the danger and long hours involved.

Children can sense the family tension caused by various hardships—work-related stress, money worries, and disagreements. Often, young children blame themselves for family crises and try to "fix" the family's problems. Children need to learn that families who love one another pull together when the going gets tough. Use this lesson to teach children that families help each other out of love, and that God's love can overcome any difficulty.

Another Scripture used in this lesson is Galatians 6:2.

Getting the Point

✏ **Families help each other in hard times.**

It's important to say The Point just as it's written in each activity. Repeating The Point over and over will help the children remember it and apply it to their lives.

Children will
- learn that family members help each other out of love,
- understand we can rely on God to help our families,
- teach Pockets that families help each other in hard times, and
- experience helping each other as a class "family."

✏ **The Point**

This Lesson at a Glance

Before the lesson, collect the necessary items for the activities you plan to use. Refer to the Classroom Supplies and Learning Lab Supplies columns to determine what you'll need. Remember to make photocopies of the "Today I Learned…" handout (p. 41) to send home with your children.

Section	Minutes	What Children Will Do	Classroom Supplies	Learning Lab Supplies
Welcome Time	up to 5	**Welcome!**—Receive name tags and be greeted by the teacher.	"Family Name Tags" hand-outs (p. 29), markers, pins or tape	
Let's Get Started Direct children to one or more of the Let's Get Started activities until everyone arrives.	up to 10	**Option 1: Snack Sandwiches**—Make sandwich snacks to share as a class later in the lesson. Hear how Ruth helped Naomi.	Whole-wheat bread, soft cream cheese, jam, plastic knives	
	up to 10	**Option 2: Grain Rubbings**—Make grain rubbings on paper with crayons and learn how Ruth gathered grain for her family.	Wheat or weeds with large seed heads, typing paper, newsprint, crayons	
	up to 10	**Option 3: Family Dress-Up**—Dress up like family members and talk about helping.	Adult ties, dresses, shirts, hats, glasses, bows	
Pick-Up Song	up to 5	**We Will Pick Up**—Sing a song as they pick up toys and gather for Bible-Story Time.	CD player	CD: "We Will Pick Up" (track 2)
Bible-Story Time	up to 5	**Setting the Stage**—Play a fun game to gather "grain."	Popcorn kernels, plastic spoons, paper lunch sacks, plastic sandwich bags	
	up to 5	**Bible Song and Prayer Time**—Sing a song, bring out the Bible, and pray together.	Bible, construction paper, scissors, basket or box, CD player	CD: "God's Book" (track 3), family stamp and ink pad
	up to 10	**Hear the Bible Story**—Play a popcorn game and hear how Ruth helped her family.	Bible, CD player, popcorn	Bible Big Book: Ruth (pp. 2-3), CD: "Ruth" (track 5)
	up to 10	**Do the Bible Story**—Play popcorn jacks in family groups and learn that helping makes a task easier.	Popcorn, typing paper	
Practicing the Point	up to 5	**I Can Help, Too!**—Teach Pockets to help during hard times.	Pockets the Kangaroo, small bag	
Closing	up to 5	**Time to Eat!**—Sing a song and share snack sandwiches.	Snack sandwiches from Option 1, napkins, CD player	CD: "God Made Families" (track 4)
For Extra Time		For extra-time ideas and supplies, see page 40.		

Families help each other.

Welcome Time

Welcome! (up to 5 minutes)

- Bend down to make eye contact with children as they arrive.
- Greet each child individually with an enthusiastic smile.
- Thank each child for coming to class today.
- As children arrive, ask them about last week's "Today I Learned..." discussion. Use questions such as "How did you help your family last week?" and "When are some times families share?"
- Say: **Today we're going to learn that ✏ families help each other in hard times.**
- Hand out the "Family" name tags children made in Lesson 1 and help them attach the name tags to their clothing. If some of the name tags were damaged or if some of the children weren't in class that week, have them make new name tags using the photocopiable patterns on page 29.
- Direct the children to the Let's Get Started activities you've set up.

✏ **The Point**

Let's Get Started

Set up one or more of the following activities for children to do as they arrive. After you greet each child, invite him or her to choose an activity.

Circulate among children to guide the activities and direct children's conversation toward today's lesson. Ask questions such as "How does God help families?" or "How can you help your family?"

☐ OPTION 1: Snack Sandwiches (up to 10 minutes)

Set out whole-wheat bread, a tub of soft cream cheese, jam, and plastic knives. Have children form an assembly line of groups such as the Spreaders, Jammers, Breaders, and Cutters. Spreaders spread cream cheese on the bread, then pass it to the Jammers, who spread jam over the cream cheese. Breaders add the top piece of bread to make a sandwich, and Cutters cut the sandwich into quarters. Tell children that in today's Bible story, they'll hear how Ruth gathered grain to share with Naomi. Gathering grain was hard work, but ✏ families help each other in hard times. Tell children they'll be sharing the sandwiches later in the lesson.

✏ **The Point**

✔ Be sure to have children make enough snack sandwiches for everyone. If you don't choose this option, make sandwiches before class to share in the closing.

☐ OPTION 2: Grain Rubbings (up to 10 minutes)

Before class, gather wheat or weeds with large seed heads. Make sure you have at least one plant for each child.

Set out plants, typing paper, crayons, and newsprint. Show children how to place the plant on newsprint and cover it with typing paper. Use a crayon to gently color over the plant to create a rubbing. Encourage children to work in pairs, one holding the paper on top of the plant while the other colors. Then have them switch. Tell children that today's Bible story is about how Ruth gathered heads of grain for her family's food. Ruth worked hard because she knew that ● families help each other in hard times.

● **The Point**

□ **OPTION 3: Family Dress-Up (up to 10 minutes)**

Set out dress-up clothes such as dresses, shirts, ties, glasses, hats, and bows. Invite children to dress up as their family members. As children dress up, ask questions such as "Who are you dressed as?" and "What special way does that person help your family?" Say that today's Bible story is about how Ruth helped her family through a hard time. Explain that because they love each other, ● families help each other in hard times.

● **The Point**

When everyone has arrived and you're ready to move on to the Bible-Story Time, encourage the children to finish what they're doing and get ready to clean up.

Pick-Up Song

We Will Pick Up (up to 5 minutes)

Lead children in singing "We Will Pick Up" (track 2) with the *CD* to the tune of "London Bridge." Encourage children to sing along as they help clean up the room.

If you want to include the names of all the children in your class, sing the song without the *CD* and repeat the naming section. If you choose to use the *CD*, vary the names you use each week.

Sing

We will pick up all our toys,
All our toys, all our toys.
We will pick up all our toys
And put them all away.

I see (name) picking up,
Picking up, picking up.
I see (name) picking up
And putting toys away.
(Repeat.)

Bible-Story Time

Setting the Stage (up to 5 minutes)

Tell the children you'll clap your hands to get their attention. Explain that when you clap your hands, children are to stop what they're doing, raise their

Families help each other.

hands, and focus on you. Encourage children to respond quickly so you'll have time for all the fun activities you've planned.

Before this activity, set out small paper sacks at one end of the room to be used as "grain sacks." You'll need one sack for every three children in your class.

Say: **Let's play a grain game! Pretend this room is a grainfield. First we have to plant our grain.**

You'll need a small bag of popcorn kernels and plastic sandwich bags. Let each child take a small handful of kernels and sprinkle them around the floor in a designated area. Say: **What a great job of planting! Now let's form families and gather our grain.** Form family groups of three.

Say: **Let's pick up the grain and bring it home like Ruth did. I'll give each of you a plastic spoon. When I flip the lights, you'll have 30 seconds to scoop up as much "grain" as you can on your spoon, then pour it in your family's grain sack. I'll flip the lights again when it's time to stop.** Assign each group a grain sack. Flip the lights to begin and end the game. When the game is over, ask children to sit on the floor in their family groups by their grain sacks.

Say: **You all did a wonderful job picking up the grain. Hold up your bags and give each other high fives.** Ask:

● **Why was it important to help each other as a family?** (The work went faster; it was easier; we got more that way.)

Say: **Just as you helped each other in our game, ● families help each other in hard times. Helping each other is one way families show their love. Let's see what the Bible says about helping each other.** Open to Galatians 6:2 and read aloud: **"Carry each other's burdens, and in this way you will fulfill the law of Christ."**

Say: **Our Bible story today is about how Ruth helped her family during a hard time. Ruth and Naomi had a hard time getting enough food. Let's hear how they helped each other through a hard time.**

● The Point

Bible Song and Prayer Time (up to 5 minutes)

Before class, make surprise cards for this activity by cutting construction paper into 2×6-inch slips. Prepare a surprise card for each child plus a few extras for visitors. Fold the cards in half, then stamp the *family stamp* inside one of the surprise cards. Mark Ruth 1:19–2:3 in the Bible you'll be using.

Have children sit in a circle with their family groups from "Setting the Stage." Say: **Now it's time to choose a Bible person to bring me the Bible marked with today's Bible story. As we sing our Bible song, I'll pass out the surprise cards. Don't look inside your card until the song is over.**

Lead children in singing "God's Book" (track 3) with the *CD* to the tune of "Old MacDonald Had a Farm." As you sing, pass out the folded surprise cards. If you want to include the names of all the children in your class, sing the song without the *CD* and repeat the naming section. If you choose to use the *CD*, vary the names you use each week.

Sing

Now it's time to read God's Book	Now it's time to read God's Book
And hear a Bible story.	And hear a Bible story.
It's fun to be here with my friends	It's fun to be here with my friends
And hear a Bible story.	And hear a Bible story.
(Name)'s here.	(Name)'s here.
(Name)'s here.	(Name)'s here.
Here is (name).	Here is (name).
Here is (name).	Here is (name).
Now it's time to read God's Book	Now it's time to read God's Book
And hear a Bible story.	And hear a Bible story.

After the song, say: **You may look inside your surprise cards. The person who has the family stamped inside his or her card will be our Bible person for today.**

Identify the Bible person, then have the rest of the children clap for him or her. Ask the Bible person to bring you the Bible. Help the Bible person open the Bible to the marked place and show children where your story comes from. Then have the Bible person sit down.

Say: (Name) **was our special Bible person today. Each week we'll have only one Bible person, but each one of you is a special part of our class! Today we're all learning that** ◖ **families help each other in hard times.**

Let's say a special prayer now and ask God to help us learn how families help each other. I'll pass around this basket. When the basket comes to you, put your surprise card in it and say, "God, please teach me to help my family in hard times.

Pass around the basket or box. When you've collected everyone's surprise card, set the basket aside and pick up the Bible. Lead children in this prayer: **God, thank you for the Bible and all the stories in it. Teach us today that** ◖ **families help each other in hard times. In Jesus' name we pray, amen.**

Hear the Bible Story (up to 10 minutes)

Bring out the Bible, *Bible Big Book: Ruth,* popped popcorn, the *CD,* and CD player. Gather children in front of the family tree for the Bible story. Hold up the Bible. Say: **Our story today comes from the book of Ruth in the Bible.** Hold up the Big Book. Say: **Our Big Book shows us pictures of the story.** Open the *Bible Big Book* to page 1. Show the picture to children as you say: **Last time we heard how Ruth and Naomi decided to go back to Bethlehem.** Point to the leaves on the bulletin board and say: **The only leaves left on the tree are for Ruth, Naomi, and God. God helped them arrive safely in Bethlehem, just in time for the grain harvest. They were so tired and hungry. Today's lesson is about how Ruth helped her family through a hard time.**

Open the *Bible Big Book* to pages 2 and 3. Show the picture to children as you say: **Ruth's work gathering grain was very important. Without grain, Ruth and Naomi wouldn't have had enough to eat. You can help me tell the Bible story, but first you'll need some popcorn.** Give each child six

The Point

The Point

pieces of popcorn. **As you hear the Bible story, listen for the word "grain." Whenever you hear the word "grain," eat a piece of popcorn.**

Have children listen to the segment of the Bible story (track 5) on the *CD.*

Turn off the *CD.* Say: **You all did a great job of listening. Ruth and Naomi faced hard times together. But God helped them, and they helped each other.** Ask:

● **How do you think Ruth and Naomi felt when they got to Bethlehem?** (Tired; scared; hungry.)

● **How did God take care of Ruth and Naomi?** (He kept them safe on their walk; they got to Bethlehem in time for the harvest; he helped them get food.)

● **Why did Ruth work so hard for Naomi?** (She loved her; they were part of the same family; they were hungry.)

Say: **Even though working in the fields was very hard for Ruth, she did it because she loved Naomi. God helped Ruth be strong. Ruth knew that ✏ families help each other in hard times. Let's play a fun game to show how families can help—even in hard times!**

Do the Bible Story (up to 10 minutes)

Have children sit on the floor in their family groups from "Setting the Stage." Say: **We're going to play jacks—with popcorn! I'll give each "family" a set of popcorn jacks. For a ball, we'll wad up a piece of paper.** Give each family group six pieces of popcorn to use as jacks and a piece of paper to wad up for the ball. Say: **One of you in each family will toss the "ball" gently into the air. Another will catch the ball before it hits the floor. And the other will pick up the jacks. On the first toss, pick up one jack and set it aside. On the second toss, pick up two jacks. And on the third toss, pick up the rest of the jacks.** Demonstrate how to toss the ball and pick up the jacks. Let children practice a few times before beginning the game.

When all the jacks are picked up, bring the families together in a circle and say: **You did a great job helping as families! Each of you helped in a special way. And each time the ball was tossed, the game got a little harder.** Ask:

● **What was it like helping each other in the game?** (It made things easier; it made it more fun.)

● **What would the game have been like if you hadn't had any help?** (It would have been harder; I couldn't have done it myself.)

Say: **That's right. The game would have been much harder to play by yourselves. But by helping each other, you were able to pick up all the jacks. Ruth and Naomi knew that helping was important. They knew that ✏ families help each other in hard times. Let's see if our friend Pockets knows how to help in hard times.**

● The Point

Families help each other.

Lesson 2 ● 37

Practicing the Point

I Can Help, Too! (up to 5 minutes)

Before class, have ready a small bag for Pockets to carry. A bag with handles would be best, to put over Pockets' arm. Crumple some paper inside the bag to make it look full.

Have children sit in a circle. Take out Pockets the Kangaroo and go through the following script. When you finish the script, put Pockets out of sight.

I Can Help, Too!

PUPPET SCRIPT

Pockets: *(Carrying small bag)* Hi, everyone! 'Bye, everyone!

Teacher: Hi and 'bye? What do you mean, Pockets? And what do you have in that bag?

Pockets: All my stuff. I've got my toothbrush, and my little bear, and my jammies. I'm going to go stay in my treehouse. *(Pockets starts to leave.)*

Teacher: Pockets, wait a minute. Why do you want to do that? How would your family feel?

Pockets: Oh, nobody'll miss me. They're too busy. I spend most of my time with the baby sitter, anyway.

Teacher: Well, I know your parents have been working a lot lately, but . . .

Pockets: And they're tired all the time—they never have time to play with me, or read to me, or anything.

● The Point

Teacher: Pockets, even though they can't spend as much time with you as they'd like, they love you very much. In our Bible story today, we learned that ● families help each other in hard times. Children, who can tell Pockets how Ruth helped her family? *(Encourage children to say how Ruth gathered grain in the fields.)* Maybe you could help your family, too.

Pockets: What could I do to help? I'm just a kid.

Teacher: Children, can you share with Pockets some ways you help your families? *(Encourage children to tell Pockets how they help at home.)*

Pockets: Hey! I could do those things, too! I guess I was being selfish and feeling sorry for myself. I'm gonna go home to help right now! Thanks for teaching me about helping. 'Bye everyone!

(Have children say goodbye to Pockets.)

Families help each other.

TODAY I LEARNED...

We believe that Christian education extends beyond the classroom into the home. Photocopy the "Today I Learned..." handout (p. 41) for this week and send it home with your children. Encourage parents to use the handout to plan meaningful family activities to reinforce this week's topic. Follow up the "Today I Learned..." activities next week by asking children what their families did.

Closing

Time to Eat! (up to 5 minutes)

You'll need the snack sandwiches from Option 1. Have children form their family groups.

Say: **Today we learned that families help each other in hard times.** Ask:

● **How did you like staying in family groups today?** (It was fun; it made things easier; I liked it.)

Say: **Let's form a circle and sing the song we learned last time, "God Made Families."** Lead children in singing "God Made Families" (track 4) with the *CD* to the tune of "Frère Jacques."

● **The Point**

Sing

God made families. *(Hand extended to heaven.)*

God made families. *(Hand extended to heaven.)*

To show his love. *(Hand to heart.)*

To show his love. *(Hand to heart.)*

We can stick together. *(All join hands.)*

We can help each other. *(All join hands.)*

And show God's love. *(Swing hands together.)*

And show God's love.

Say: **As families today, we've worked, played, and helped each other. Another thing families do together is share meals. Ruth and Naomi enjoyed sharing the bread they made. Let's share the snack sandwiches we made together.**

Pass around the plate of snack-sandwich quarters from Option 1. Say: **Let's say a prayer before we eat.** Pray: **Thank you, God, for giving us food and friends to share it with.**

After children finish eating, say: **Let's say a prayer before we go home.** Pray: **Dear God, thank you for our families and for all the things our families do to take care of us. Help us remember that families help each other in hard times. In Jesus' name we pray, amen.**

● **The Point**

For Extra Time

If you have a long class time or want to add additional elements to your lesson, try one of the following activities.

LIVELY LEARNING: Separating the Grain

Before class, fold several paper fans from construction paper.

Set out a small bowl of dry lima beans, cotton balls, several pieces of brown construction paper, and the fans. Explain to children that part of harvesting in Bible times was to separate the grain from the stems. Workers tossed the mixture up into the air—the grain fell and the stems blew away in the wind.

Form groups of three. Give each group a fan, a piece of brown paper to be the threshing floor, two lima beans to be the wheat, and two cotton balls to be the chaff. Put the lima beans and cotton balls on the brown paper and have two children lift the paper. The third child will use the fan to blow the cotton balls away from the beans, as workers in Bible times separated the wheat from the chaff. Talk about how hard it was for Ruth to work in the fields, and remind children that ⬤ families help each other in hard times.

⬤ **The Point**

MAKE TO TAKE: Family Streamers

Before class, cut a sheet of construction paper into quarters for each child. Also, cut at least four 2-foot lengths of ribbon for each child. Set out paper squares, ribbon, tape, scissors, and markers to make family streamers. Have children use markers to draw pictures of their families on the paper squares. Help children tape each picture to a ribbon. Then have them tie their ribbons together at the top. Encourage children to hang their streamers at home by a window or door where they'll blow in the breeze. Remind children we're all part of God's family and that ⬤ families help each other in hard times.

⬤ **The Point**

TREAT TO EAT: Edible Family Trees

Before class, cut enough small cheese cubes and broccoli "trees" for each member of your class. Give each child a cheese cube and a broccoli tree. Direct children to push the broccoli trunk into the cheese so it will stand. Review the family tree used in the lesson. Remind children that Ruth helped Naomi through a hard time and that ⬤ families help each other in hard times.

⬤ **The Point**

STORY PICTURE: Ruth Gathers Grain

Give each child a photocopy of the "Today I Learned..." handout from page 41. Cover work area with newsprint. Set out brushes, glue, and small bowls of cornmeal. Have children brush glue on the grainfield in the picture and sprinkle it with cornmeal. Have them shake off the excess. As children work, remind them that Ruth worked hard to gather grain because ⬤ families help each other in hard times.

⬤ **The Point**

Families help each other.

TODAY I LEARNED...

The Point ✏ Families help each other in hard times.

Today your child learned that families help each other in hard times. Children learned that Ruth helped Naomi by gathering grain for food. Children talked about how to help their own families in hard times.

Verse to Learn

"As for me and my household, we will serve the Lord" (Joshua 24:15b).

Ask Me...

● How did Ruth help her family in hard times?
● What can you do to help your family in hard times?
● How does our family help each other?

Family Fun

● Make a family tree together. Use a large sheet of construction paper and finger paint. Let family members make their own hand-print leaves above and around the trunk. As you work together, talk about how helping each other is one way families show love.
● Choose a large task for the whole family to tackle, such as cleaning the garage or working in the yard. Divide the task into small jobs that each family member can accomplish. Celebrate with an ice-cream outing when you finish.

Ruth Gathers Grain (Ruth 1:19–2:3)

Families Share

The Bible Basis

Ruth 2:4-23. Boaz leaves grain for Ruth.

Ruth worked hard in the fields gathering grain to feed herself and her mother-in-law. Ruth's dedication and love for Naomi caught the eye of Boaz, the wealthy owner of the fields. As a kinsman, Boaz wanted to help this compassionate young Moabite widow. He told the workers to drop extra grain for Ruth and not send her away. And in an act of gentle compassion, Boaz shared his own food and water with Ruth and warned his workers not to bother her.

Sharing can be difficult for 5- and 6-year-olds. The stuffed dog that a child hasn't played with for weeks suddenly becomes a prized possession when a sibling or friend wants to play with it! Sharing is OK if the desired item belongs to someone else, or if the sharing involves yummy treats or a fun day at the zoo. Children need to recognize that when they share in the fun things, they need to share in family responsibilities as well. It's important for young children to understand that we share because we love each other, and that God wants us to share with our families.

Getting the Point

✎**Families help each other and share with each other.**

It's important to say The Point just as it's written in each activity. Repeating The Point over and over will help the children remember it and apply it to their lives.

Children will
- learn that families share with each other,
- realize that sharing is one way to show love,
- help Pockets understand that giving is more fun than receiving, and
- understand that when we share with others, they want to share with us.

✎ **The Point**

This Lesson at a Glance

Before the lesson, collect the necessary items for the activities you plan to use. Refer to the Classroom Supplies and Learning Lab Supplies columns to determine what you'll need. Remember to make photocopies of the "Today I learned..." handout (p. 54) to send home with your children.

Section	Minutes	What Children Will Do	Classroom Supplies	Learning Lab Supplies
Welcome Time	up to 5	**Welcome!**—Receive name tags and be greeted by the teacher.	"Family Name Tags" handouts (p. 29), markers, pins or tape	
Let's Get Started Direct children to one or more of the Let's Get Started activities until everyone arrives.	up to 10	**Option 1: Crayon Pair Share**—Share crayons and make family pictures.	Crayons, rubber bands, paper	Cape, family stamp and ink pad
	up to 10	**Option 2: Robe Decoration**—Decorate a colorful cape to help tell the Bible story.	Markers, glue sticks, sequins, ribbon, crayons	
	up to 10	**Option 3: Share Square**—Walk, hop, and balance on masking tape square.	Masking tape	
Pick-Up Song	up to 5	**We Will Pick Up**—Sing a song as they pick up toys and gather for Bible-Story Time.	CD player	CD: "We Will Pick Up" (track 2)
Bible-Story Time	up to 5	**Setting the Stage**—Build with straws and learn how sharing makes families stronger.	Plastic drinking straws, masking tape, a few books	
	up to 5	**Bible Song and Prayer Time**—Sing a song, bring out the Bible, and pray together.	Bible, construction paper, scissors, basket or box, CD player	CD: "God's Book" (track 3), family stamp and ink pad
	up to 10	**Hear the Bible Story**—Act out the Bible story using the decorated cape.	Bible, Family Tree and Story Faces leaves from Lesson 1	Bible Big Book: Ruth (pp. 4-5), cape
	up to 10	**Do the Bible Story**—Participate in a cooperative wheelbarrow game.		Family stamp and ink pad
Practicing the Point	up to 5	**Ticket Tangle**—Help Pockets learn about family sharing.	Pockets the Kangaroo, 3x5 cards	
Closing	up to 5	**Share the News**—Talk about sharing and sing a song.	CD player	CD: "My Own Family" (track 6)
For Extra Time	For extra-time ideas and supplies, see page 53.			

Families help each other.

Welcome Time

Welcome! (up to 5 minutes)

- Bend down to make eye contact with children as they arrive.
- Greet each child individually with an enthusiastic smile.
- Thank each child for coming to class today.
- As children arrive, ask them about last week's "Today I Learned..." discussion. Ask questions such as "How did you help your family last week?" and "What was one difficult thing you did last week? How did your family help you?"
- Say: **Today we're going to learn that ● families help each other and share with each other.**
- Hand out the "Family" name tags children made during Lesson 1 and help them attach the name tags to their clothing. If some of the name tags were damaged or if children weren't in class that week, have them make new name tags using the photocopiable handout on page 29.
- Direct the children to the Let's Get Started activities you've set up.

● **The Point**

Let's Get Started

Set up one or more of the following activities for children to do as they arrive. After you greet each child, invite him or her to choose an activity.

Circulate among children to guide the activities and direct children's conversation toward today's lesson. Ask questions such as "How do families share with each other?" or "What are some ways God shares his love with your family?"

OPTION 1: Crayon Pair Share (up to 10 minutes)

Before class, secure pairs of crayons together with rubber bands.

Set out the crayon pairs. As children arrive, hand each one a sheet of paper and a pair of crayons. Invite children to draw colorful pictures of something their family shares, such as meals or vacations in the car. Encourage the children to share their crayons when they want to use a new color. Reinforce sharing with comments such as "It's fun to share because then we have more" and "Sharing with our families is a good way to show our love." Remind children that ● families help each other and share with each other. Say that today's Bible story is about a man named Boaz. Explain that Boaz was really part of Ruth's family. Point out that just as they shared their crayons, Boaz shared with his family.

● **The Point**

OPTION 2: Cape Decoration (up to 10 minutes)

Set out the *cape, family stamp and ink pad,* markers, crayons, glue sticks, and other decorations such as sequins, ribbon, or colored tissue paper.

Invite children to decorate the *cape* from the Learning Lab. As children

The Point work, point out that women in Bible times made clothing for everyone in their families. Tell children that in the Bible story today they'll learn another way Ruth's family shared. Point out that  families help each other and share with each other. Explain they'll get a chance to share the *cape* and help tell the Bible story.

When children are finished decorating the *cape,* set it aside for the Bible-Story Time.

☐ Option 3: Share Square (up to 10 minutes)

Before class, use masking tape to make a 4-foot square on the floor.

Have each child find a partner and stand on one side of the square. If you have more than eight children in your class, make another square on the floor. Invite children to hop, balance, and walk backward and forward. Challenge children to walk in different directions around the square and pass one another without stepping off the tape. Encourage children to help each other keep their balance. Explain that just as they're helping each other to share the square, ● families help each other and share with each other.

The Point

When everyone has arrived and you're ready to move on to the Bible-Story Time, encourage the children to finish what they're doing and get ready to clean up.

Pick-Up Song

We Will Pick Up (up to 5 minutes)

Lead children in singing "We Will Pick Up" (track 2) with the *CD* to the tune of "London Bridge." Encourage the children to sing along as they help clean up the room.

If you want to include the names of all the children in your class, sing the song without the *CD.* If you choose to use the *CD,* vary the names you use each week.

Sing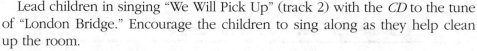

We will pick up all our toys,
All our toys, all our toys.
We will pick up all our toys
And put them all away.

I see (name) picking up,
Picking up, picking up.
I see (name) picking up
And putting toys away.

(Repeat.)

Families help each other.

Bible-Story Time

Setting the Stage (up to 5 minutes)

Tell the children you'll clap your hands to get their attention. Explain that when you clap your hands, children are to stop what they're doing, raise their hands, and focus on you. Encourage children to respond quickly so you'll have time for all the fun activities you've planned.

Set out a box of plastic drinking straws, a roll of masking tape, and a few books. Hand each child a drinking straw. Ask:

● **What do you think will happen if we balance a book on one straw?** (The book will fall; the straw will bend or break; the straw's not strong enough.)

Encourage children to try balancing books on their straws.

Then form two family groups. Say: **Help your family group think of a way to make the straws strong enough to hold books.** Give hints such as "Would the straws be stronger together?" and "How could we fasten them together?" Let children use the masking tape to fasten their straws together.

When both "families" are finished, let them try to balance books on their straws. Ask:

● **Why are many straws stronger than one?** (Because one straw is too thin and weak, and lots of straws together are thick and strong.)

● **How are we stronger as a family than we are alone?** (We can help each other; we're all good at different things.)

Say: **When we share and help each other in our families, our families grow stronger, just as all of our straws put together were stronger than one straw by itself. It's good when ✏ families help each other and share with each other. Today's Bible story is about how Ruth's family helped each other and shared.**

Bible Song and Prayer Time (up to 5 minutes)

Before class, make surprise cards for this activity by cutting construction paper into 2×6-inch slips. Prepare a surprise card for each child plus a few extras for visitors. Fold the cards in half, then stamp the *family stamp* inside one of the surprise cards. Mark Ruth 2:4-23 in the Bible you'll be using.

Have children sit in a circle. Say: **Now it's time to choose a Bible person to bring me the Bible marked with today's Bible story. As we sing our Bible song, I'll pass out the surprise cards. Don't look inside your card until the song is over.**

Lead children in singing "God's Book" (track 3) with the *CD* to the tune of "Old MacDonald Had a Farm." As you sing, pass out the folded surprise cards. If you want to include the names of all the children in your class, sing the song without the *CD* and repeat the naming section. If you choose to use the *CD,* vary the names you use each week.

✏ **The Point**

Sing

Now it's time to read God's Book
And hear a Bible story.
It's fun to be here with my
  friends
And hear a Bible story.
	Now it's time to read God's Book
	And hear a Bible story.
	It's fun to be here with my
	  friends
	And hear a Bible story.

(Name)'s here. (Name)'s here. Here is (name). Here is (name). Now it's time to read God's Book And hear a Bible story.	(Name)'s here. (Name)'s here. Here is (name). Here is (name). Now it's time to read God's Book And hear a Bible story.

After the song, say: **You may look inside your surprise cards. The person who has the family stamped inside his or her card will be our Bible person for today.**

Identify the Bible person, then have the rest of the children clap for him or her. Ask the Bible person to bring you the Bible. Help the Bible person open the Bible to the marked place and show children where your story comes from. Then have the Bible person sit down.

Say: (Name) **was our special Bible person today. Each week we'll have only one Bible person, but each one of you is a special part of our class!**

🖊 The Point

Today we're all learning that 🖊 families help each other and share with each other.

Let's say a special prayer now and ask God to teach us to share with our families. I'll pass around this basket. When the basket comes to you, put your surprise card in it and say, "God, please teach me to share with my family."

Pass around the basket or box. When you've collected everyone's surprise card, set the basket aside and pick up the Bible. Lead children in this prayer:

🖊 The Point

God, thank you for the Bible and all the stories in it. Teach us today that 🖊 families help each other and share with each other. In Jesus' name we pray, amen.

Hear the Bible Story (up to 10 minutes)

Before this activity, tape the Story Faces leaves from Lesson 1 back on the family tree.

Gather children in front of the family tree for the Bible story. Hold up the Bible. Say: **Our story today comes from the Bible.** Hold up the *Bible Big Book: Ruth.* Say: **Our Big Book shows us pictures of the story. Before we begin, let's use the family tree to play a review game. I'll ask a story question. If you know the answer, pose like a tree—like this.** Demonstrate how to stand straight with your arms out like branches and your fingers waving like leaves. **Then I'll call on someone to answer the question and point to the correct story leaf on the bulletin board.**

Use the following questions to review the last two lessons.
- **Who was Naomi's husband?** (Elimelech.)
- **How many sons did Naomi have?** (Two.)

Families help each other.

- **Who married Naomi's sons?** (Orpah and Ruth.)
- **Who died in Moab? Remove their leaves.** (Remove the leaves with the pictures of Elimelech and his two sons.)
- **Who stayed behind when Ruth and Naomi left for Bethlehem? Remove her leaf from the tree.** (Orpah.)
- **Whose leaves are left on the tree?** (Ruth, Naomi, and God.)

Say: **You all did a great job of remembering. Let's clap for each other.** Pause for children to respond. **Last time we heard how Ruth gathered grain to help her family. God watched over Ruth as she gathered grain. But someone else was watching her, too. Let's add a story leaf for Boaz, the person who watched Ruth.** Add the leaf with the picture of Boaz on it to the family tree.

Say: **In our Bible story today, we'll find out that sharing is a good way to show you care about someone. We'll use the *cape* to act out the Bible story. Let's sit in a circle. We'll pass the *cape* around the circle as I read from the *Bible Big Book.* If you're holding the *cape* when I say the name "Naomi," hold the *cape* on your head like an old woman's scarf. If you're holding the *cape* when I say the name "Boaz," hold the *cape* around your shoulders like a man's cape. And if you're holding the *cape* when I say the name "Ruth," hold the *cape* around your waist like a woman's skirt. Then pass the *cape* to the person next to you.**

Take out the *Bible Big Book* and show children pages 4 and 5. Read the text for those pages from the back cover, pausing each time you mention the names of Ruth, Naomi, and Boaz.

Close the Big Book when the story is finished. Return the *cape* to the Learning Lab. Say: **You did a great job listening and using the *cape* to act out the Bible story. Let's see what you remember.** Ask:
- **Who was watching Ruth?** (Boaz; God.)
- **What did Boaz share with Ruth?** (His food and water; his grain.)
- **Why did Boaz share with Ruth?** (They were from the same family; he liked her.)

Say: **Boaz and Ruth were from the same family. And because families love each other, Boaz shared with Ruth.** Ask:
- **What does your family share?** (Our food; our house; love; our money.)
- **What would it be like if your family didn't share?** (Bad; sad; mean.)

Say: **Boaz wanted to help Ruth, so he shared with her. He knew that ⬤ families help each other and share with each other. Let's play a game to see how families share.**

⬤ **The Point**

Do the Bible Story (up to 10 minutes)

Form groups of three. Say: **Decide who in your group will be the Wheelbarrow and who will be the two Handles. Each Handle can carry a leg of the Wheelbarrow while the Wheelbarrow walks his or her hands across the room to the wall and back. Don't "push" the Wheelbarrow, just work together to get to the wall. When I flip the lights, you can go.**

When each group is back at the starting place, ask:
- **What was it like working together?** (It was fun; it was hard.)

● **How did you help each other?** (We each carried a leg; the Handles helped the Wheelbarrow walk.)

● **Could the Wheelbarrows have made it across the room without help? Explain.** (Not very easily, because they needed the Handles to hold them.)

Say: **Just like families share and help each other, you helped each other finish the race. You can stamp your hands with the** *family stamp* **to help**  **The Point** **you remember that** ⬤**families help each other and share with each other. Now let's see how our friend Pockets shares with her family.**

Practicing the Point

Ticket Tangle (up to 5 minutes)

Before class, make four pretend tickets by cutting two 3×5 cards in half. Write the words "Kangaroo Fun Land" on each ticket. Slide the tickets in Pockets' pouch.

Have children sit in a circle. Take out Pockets the Kangaroo and go through the following script. When you finish the script, put Pockets out of sight.

Ticket Tangle

PUPPET SCRIPT

Pockets: Hi, everyone! Look what I've got in my pocket!

Teacher: Hi, Pockets! *(Looks at tickets.)* Wow! Tickets to Kangaroo Fun Land.

Pockets: *(Nods enthusiastically.)* I won four free tickets at the grocery store. I'm going this weekend. I can't wait to ride on the Twirly, Whirly, Super Swirly Roller Coaster! *(Leans back and forth like she's riding a roller coaster.)* Zooooom! What's your favorite ride?

(Let children tell about their favorite carnival rides.)

Teacher: It sounds like you'll have a great time, Pockets. Who's going with you?

Pockets: *(Scratches her head.)* I don't know! I have three extra tickets, but I can't decide who to take.

Teacher: Why not invite your family to go?

Pockets: My <u>family</u>?

Teacher: Yes, your family! It would be fun. And it would be a great way to share with your family. Children, can you tell Pockets how Boaz shared with his family? *(Encourage children to tell Pockets how Boaz shared grain, food, and water. Encourage them to tell Pockets The Point and that sharing is a way to show your family love.)*

(Continued)

Families help each other.

Teacher: Families share because they love each other.

Pockets: *(Nods yes.)* And Mom and Dad really do like the rides. And my little sister has never been to Fun Land before. And we could share cotton candy! *(Rubs her tummy.)* Mmmm, mmmm! I think I will share with my family! Thanks for helping me learn that ✏ families help each other and share with each other.

(Have children say goodbye to Pockets.)

✏ **The Point**

TODAY I LEARNED...

We believe that Christian education extends beyond the classroom into the home. Photocopy the "Today I Learned..." handout (p. 54) for this week and send it home with your children. Encourage parents to use the handout to plan meaningful family activities to reinforce this week's topic. Follow up the "Today I Learned..." activities next week by asking children what their families did.

Closing

Share the News (up to 5 minutes)

Form pairs. Say: **Today we learned that ✏ families help each other and share with each other. Let's join hands with our partners and tell each other a way families share.**

When children have all told ways that families share, say: **Now each pair join hands with another pair, and everyone tell one way you can share with your family this week.**

When everyone's told a way to share, say: **I know your families will appreciate your sharing this week. Let's sing a song about our families.** Lead children in singing "My Own Family" (track 6) with the *CD* to the tune of "Old MacDonald Had a Farm." For extra fun, join hands and walk or hop in a circle as you sing.

✏ **The Point**

Sing

I'm so glad to be a part
Of my own fam-i-ly. *(Clap, clap.)*
We help and share in all we do,
In my own fam-i-ly. *(Clap, clap.)*
Parents, brother, sister, too,
Grandma, grandpa
I love you.
I'm so glad to be a part
Of my own fam-i-ly. *(Clap, clap.)*

I'm so glad to be a part
Of my own fam-i-ly. *(Clap, clap.)*
We celebrate our love for God
In my own fam-i-ly. *(Clap, clap.)*
Parents, brother, sister, too,
Grandma, grandpa
I love you.
I'm so glad to be a part
Of my own fam-i-ly. *(Clap, clap.)*

The Point

After the song, ask children to sit on the floor. Say: **We had fun today as part of God's family! Just as Boaz shared with his family, we've learned to share with our families, too. Before you go, let's pray together.** Pray: **Dear God, thank you for our families. Help us remember that ⬤ families help each other and share with each other. In Jesus' name we pray, amen.**

For Extra Time

If you have a long class time or want to add additional elements to your lesson, try one of the following activities.

LIVELY LEARNING: Sled Rides

In Bible times, sleds were sometimes used to thresh the wheat. Before class, make a small sled for this activity. You'll need a corrugated cardboard box big enough for a child to sit in, and two 3-foot pieces of rope for each sled. Make two holes in the front of each box, midway up, a few inches from either side. Reinforce the area around the holes with duct tape. Put the rope through the holes and knot on the inside. Let children take turns riding in the sled as the others pull the sled around the "field."

MAKE TO TAKE: String Fields

Before class, cut string into 4-inch pieces. You'll need several pieces for each child in your class. Cover work area with newsprint. Set out markers, lengths of string, butcher paper, and bowls of brown and yellow tempera paint mixed with a little soap. Give each child a piece of paper and a few pieces of string. Help children make grain-stalk pictures by dipping string into the paint and laying it on one side of the paper. Fold the paper in half over the string and press down. Open the paper and remove strings to reveal painted stalks. Use markers to draw grain on the stalks, or use the ink pad and make thumb-print seeds.

TREAT TO EAT: Cornmeal Pancakes

Set out an electric skillet, a bowl, a spatula, corn bread mix, and ingredients. As the skillet is heating, have children take turns adding and mixing the ingredients. Cook the batter as you would pancakes. Tell children to pretend they are working as a family to make a meal. Remind them that ●families help each other and share with each other. Serve the cornmeal pancakes on paper plates. As children are eating, talk about different foods made from grain, such as cereals, bread, and cakes.

● The Point

STORY PICTURE: Boaz Leaves Extra Grain for Ruth

Give each child a photocopy of the "Today I Learned..." handout from page 54. Set out glue and pieces of burlap. Children will glue burlap pieces to the grain bags. As children work, talk about ways families help each other.

TODAY I LEARNED...

The Point 🖊 Families help each other and share with each other.

LESSON 3

Today your child learned that families help each other and share with each other. Children learned how Boaz shared his grain and provisions with Ruth. They talked about ways they can share with their families.

Verse to Learn

"As for me and my household, we will serve the Lord" (Joshua 24:15b).

Ask Me...

● How did Boaz help Ruth?
● How can you share with your family?
● What are some ways families share with each other?

Family Fun

● Let your child help make a Boaz Breakfast to share just as Boaz shared with Ruth. Fix whole-grain toast sprinkled with "love" (cinnamon), "helping ham and eggs" or pancakes, and "sharing syrup." Talk about how love, helping, and sharing are things God wants families to do.

Boaz Shares Grain With Ruth (Ruth 2:4-23)

Families Celebrate

The Point
🖊 Families help each other and celebrate together.

The Bible Basis

Ruth 3:1–4:16. Ruth and Boaz celebrate their marriage.

Naomi loved Ruth and wanted her to find a husband and a good home. She encouraged Ruth to lie at Boaz's feet, as was the Jewish custom when a woman sought a kinsman's protection through marriage. Obediently, Ruth went to the threshing floor and lay at Boaz's feet. Boaz woke, and when he saw that it was Ruth, he understood her plea for protection. The marriage of Ruth and Boaz must have been quite a celebration. The new family brought comfort and eventually a grandchild to Naomi. The child, Obed, became the grandfather of David, Israel's greatest king, and part of the family line of Jesus.

Family celebrations are memory makers for children. Five- and 6-year-olds love planning for and helping with family events. Often, the happiness and family closeness fostered in the child outlast the glow of the event itself. Use this lesson to teach children that families can celebrate good times and God's love together.

Getting the Point

🖊**Families help each other and celebrate together.**

It's important to say The Point just as it's written in each activity. Repeating The Point over and over will help the children remember it and apply it to their lives.

Children will
● learn that families share happy times,
● celebrate God's love,
● help Pockets plan a surprise party, and
● enjoy a class party together.

🖊 **The Point**

This Lesson at a Glance

Before the lesson, collect the necessary items for the activities you plan to use. Refer to the Classroom Supplies and Learning Lab Supplies columns to determine what you'll need. Remember to make photocopies of the "Today I Learned..." handout (p. 66) to send home with your children.

Section	Minutes	What Children Will Do	Classroom Supplies	Learning Lab Supplies
Welcome Time	up to 5	**Welcome!**—Receive name tags and be greeted by the teacher.	"Family Name Tags" handouts (p. 29), markers, pins or tape	
Let's Get Started Direct children to one or more of the Let's Get Started activities until everyone arrives.	up to 10	**Option 1: Wedding Bells**—Make surprise sacks to share with their families.	"Wedding Bells" handouts (p. 65), paper lunch sacks, tape, scissors, erasers, stickers	
	up to 10	**Option 2: Party Table**—Decorate a party table to use for class celebration.	Shelf paper, tape, markers, construction paper, a paper punch, scissors	
	up to 10	**Option 3: Party Hats**—Make unusual party hats like Ruth and Boaz might have worn.	Paper towels, tape, scissors, construction paper	
Pick-Up Song	up to 5	**We Will Pick Up**—Sing a song as they pick up toys and gather for Bible-Story Time.	CD player	CD: "We Will Pick Up" (track 2)
Bible-Story Time	up to 5	**Setting the Stage**—Decorate special party cupcakes to share.	Cupcakes, canned icing, sprinkles, raisins, plastic knives	
	up to 5	**Bible Song and Prayer Time**—Sing a song, bring out the Bible, and pray together.	Bible, construction paper, scissors, basket or box, CD player	CD: "God's Book" (track 3), family stamp and ink pad
	up to 10	**Hear the Bible Story**—Use party balloons to help tell the Bible story.	Bible, CD player, balloons, Family Tree from Lesson 1	Bible Big Book: Ruth (pp. 6-8), CD: "Ruth" (track 7)
	up to 10	**Do the Bible Story**—Sing a song and play a fun balloon game.	Balloons from "Hear the Bible Story," tape, CD player	CD: "My Own Family" (track 6)
Practicing the Point	up to 5	**Pockets Plans a Party**—Help Pockets with decoration ideas for a surprise party.	Pockets the Kangaroo, balloons	
Closing	up to 5	**Party Time**—Celebrate being a class family.	Cupcakes from "Setting the Stage," napkins	
For Extra Time		For extra-time ideas and supplies, see page 64.		

Families help each other.

Welcome Time

Welcome! (up to 5 minutes)

- Bend down to make eye contact with children as they arrive.
- Greet each child individually with an enthusiastic smile.
- Thank each child for coming to class today.
- As children arrive, ask them about last week's "Today I Learned..." discussion. Ask questions such as "What did you share with your family last week?" and "How did you feel when you shared with your family?"
- Say: **Today we're going to learn that ⬤ families help each other and celebrate together.**
- Hand out the "Family" name tags children made during Lesson 1 and help them attach the name tags to their clothing. If some of the name tags were damaged or if children weren't in class that week, have them make new name tags using the photocopiable patterns on page 29.
- Direct children to the Let's Get Started activities you've set up.

⬤ **The Point**

Let's Get Started

Set up one or more of the following activities for children to do as they arrive. After you greet each child, invite him or her to choose an activity.

Circulate among children to guide the activities and direct children's conversation toward today's lesson. Ask questions such as "When do families celebrate together?" or "How do you help your family celebrate?"

OPTION 1: Wedding Bells (up to 10 minutes)

Before class, photocopy the "Wedding Bells" handout on page 65. You'll need two bells for each member of your class. Set out paper lunch sacks, tape, scissors, and small favors such as erasers and stickers. Invite children to make wedding-bell surprise sacks to share with their families. Form three groups: Careful Cutters, Sack Stuffers, and Bell Ringers. Careful Cutters cut out wedding bells from the handouts. Sack Stuffers evenly distribute the items among the sacks, then fold down and tape the tops. Bell Ringers tape a wedding bell to both sides of each sack.

Tell children that today they'll hear a Bible story about a big wedding celebration. Explain that the class will celebrate today, too. Tell children they can take their wedding-bell sacks home to remind them that ⬤ families help each other and celebrate together.

⬤ **The Point**

OPTION 2: Party Table (up to 10 minutes)

Before class, cover a table with white shelf paper or newsprint.

Set out tape, scissors, construction paper, markers, and a paper punch. Invite children to help turn the plain table into a party table. Show them how to make confetti using the paper punch and construction paper. Encourage them to create colorful streamers by cutting construction paper strips and taping them to the table. Let children draw pretty squiggles and other decorations with the markers.

As children work, explain that parties are one way for families to celebrate special times like weddings, birthdays, and holidays. Ask children to tell about happy times or parties their families have shared. Tell them that ⬤ families help each other and celebrate together and that today they'll hear how Ruth and Boaz celebrated their wedding day.

⬤ **The Point**

⬤ **The Point**

OPTION 3: Party Hats (up to 10 minutes)

Set out construction paper, scissors, tape, and paper towels. Help children make headbands using strips of construction paper. Tape the ends together to fit around their heads. Show children how to tape paper towels inside the back of the headbands so the towels hang down.

As children work, ask questions such as "What do you like to wear to parties?" and "Why do families have parties?" Explain that ⬤ families help each other and celebrate together in many special ways. Tell children that today's Bible story is about how Ruth and Boaz celebrated their wedding. Explain that the hats they're making are similar to what people may have worn to parties in Bible times.

If all children didn't choose to do Option 3, have volunteers make extra party hats to share. Be sure children's names are written on their hats. Then set the hats aside until later.

When everyone has arrived and you're ready to move on to the Bible-Story Time, encourage children to finish what they're doing and get ready to clean up.

Pick-Up Song

We Will Pick Up (up to 5 minutes)

Lead children in singing "We Will Pick Up" (track 2) with the *CD* to the tune of "London Bridge." Encourage children to sing along as they help clean up the room.

If you want to include the names of all the children in your class, sing the song without the *CD* and repeat the naming section. If you choose to use the *CD,* vary the names you use each week.

Sing

We will pick up all our toys,
All our toys, all our toys.
We will pick up all our toys
And put them all away.

I see (name) picking up,
Picking up, picking up.
I see (name) picking up
And putting toys away.

(Repeat.)

Families help each other.

Bible-Story Time

Setting the Stage (up to 5 minutes)

Tell the children you'll clap your hands to get their attention. Explain that when you clap your hands, children are to stop what they're doing, raise their hands, and focus on you. Encourage children to respond quickly so you'll have time for all the fun activities you've planned.

Set out a prepared cupcake for each child, plastic knives, canned icing, and small bowls of candy sprinkles or raisins. Say: **Our Bible story today is about a big celebration. Let's get ready for our own celebration, too, by decorating some party cupcakes to enjoy later. First we'll need to form two groups: the Spreaders and the Sprinklers. The Spreaders can spread icing on each cupcake, and the Sprinklers can sprinkle decorations on top.**

 ✔ You may want to decorate cookies from the store instead of cupcakes. Be sure there's a cookie for each child and a few extras for visitors.

As children work, make comments such as "Families have special party fun just like we're having fun together" and "Aren't families great to celebrate with?" When the cupcakes are finished, set them aside until the Closing activity.

Sit with the children on the floor. Ask:

● **What's your favorite family celebration?** (Christmas; birthdays; Easter; Valentine's Day.)

● **Why is it important for families to celebrate happy times?** (It's fun; it shows we love each other.)

Say: **It's fun to celebrate special times with our families. Birthdays and holidays are fun, and we can even celebrate God's love together. Isn't it great that God gave us families and that ◗ families help each other and celebrate together? Now let's hear a Bible story about a family that celebrated a wedding together.**

◗ The Point

Bible Song and Prayer Time (up to 5 minutes)

Before class, make surprise cards for this activity by cutting construction paper into 2×6-inch slips. Prepare a surprise card for each child plus a few extras for visitors. Fold the cards in half, then stamp the *family stamp* inside one of the surprise cards. Mark Ruth 3:1–4:16 in the Bible you'll be using.

Have children sit in a circle. Say: **Now it's time to choose a Bible person to bring me the Bible marked with today's Bible story. As we sing our Bible song, I'll pass out the surprise cards. Don't look inside your surprise card until the song is over.**

Lead children in singing "God's Book" (track 3) with the *CD* to the tune of "Old MacDonald Had a Farm." As you sing, pass out the folded surprise cards. If you want to include the names of all the children in your class, sing the song without the *CD* and repeat the naming section. If you choose to use the *CD*, vary the names you use each week.

Sing

Now it's time to read God's Book	Now it's time to read God's Book
And hear a Bible story.	And hear a Bible story.
It's fun to be here with my	It's fun to be here with my
friends	friends
And hear a Bible story.	And hear a Bible story.

(Name)'s **here.**	(Name)'s **here.**
(Name)'s **here.**	(Name)'s **here.**
Here is (name).	**Here is** (name).
Here is (name).	**Here is** (name).
Now it's time to read God's Book	Now it's time to read God's Book
And hear a Bible story.	And hear a Bible story.

After the song, say: **You may look inside your surprise cards. The person who has the family stamped inside his or her card will be our Bible person for today.**

Identify the Bible person, then have the rest of the children clap for him or her. Ask the Bible person to bring you the Bible. Help the Bible person open the Bible to the marked place and show children where your story comes from. Then have the Bible person sit down.

Say: (Name) **was our special Bible person today. Each week we'll have only one Bible person, but each one of you is a special part of our class! Today we'll learn that** ⬤ **families help each other and celebrate together.**

Let's say a special prayer now and ask God to help us learn how families celebrate together. I'll pass around this basket. When the basket comes to you, put your surprise card in it and say, "God, please teach me that families celebrate together."

Pass around the basket or box. When you've collected everyone's surprise card, set the basket aside and pick up the Bible. Lead children in this prayer: **God, thank you for the Bible and all the stories in it. Teach us today that** ⬤ **families help each other and celebrate together. In Jesus' name, amen.**

⬤ The Point

⬤ The Point

Hear the Bible Story (up to 10 minutes)

Before this activity, set out a bag of balloons. Gather children in front of the family tree on the bulletin board for the Bible story. Hold up the Bible. Say: **Our story today comes from the book of Ruth in the Bible.** Hold up the *Bible Big Book: Ruth*. Say: **Our *Bible Big Book* shows us pictures of the story. Before we begin, let's look at the family tree.**

Ask: **How many leaves do we have on the tree?** (Children will answer "four.") Say: **That's right, we have four leaves—one for God, one for Naomi, one for Ruth, and one for Boaz. Last time we learned how Boaz shared with Ruth. What kinds of things did he share?** (His fields; food; water.)

Say: **Those are good answers! Today our Bible story is about how Ruth and Boaz got married. They had a big party to celebrate their wedding. You can help tell the story with these party balloons.** Hand each child a balloon. **Listen to the Bible story. Girls, every time you hear the name Ruth, puff into your balloons, then pinch the ends shut to keep** the air inside. **Boys, every time you hear the name Boaz, puff into your balloons, then pinch them shut. When the story is finished, I'll help tie your balloons.**

Open the *Bible Big Book* to page 6 and listen to the "Ruth" segment (track 7) from the *CD*. Turn the page when you hear the chime. When the story is finished, close the *Bible Big Book* and set it aside.

Help children tie their balloons. Then ask:

● **Why did Naomi want Ruth to be married?** (So Ruth would have a home; so Boaz could protect her; because Naomi loved Ruth.)

● **How did Ruth and Boaz celebrate their wedding?** (With their friends; with a feast; with a party.)

● **Remember how Ruth and Naomi shared lots of hard times?** Pause for responses. **Why is it important for families to also share the good times?** (It makes them stronger; they have fun; God wants them to.)

Say: **What a happy ending to our Bible story! God blessed Ruth, Naomi, and Boaz because they helped each other. And God gave them lots to celebrate. God blesses families when  families help each other and celebrate together. Let's sing a celebration song with our balloons.**

 **The Point**

Do the Bible Story (up to 10 minutes)

Say: **Let's sing the family song we learned last week. You can bop your balloon up and down and all around as we sing.** Sing "My Own Family" (track 6) with the *CD* to the tune of "Old MacDonald Had a Farm."

Sing

I'm so glad to be a part
Of my own fam-i-ly.
We help and share in all we do,
In my own fam-i-ly.
Parents, brother, sister, too,
Grandma, grandpa
I love you.
I'm so glad to be a part
Of my own fam-i-ly.

I'm so glad to be a part
Of my own fam-i-ly.
We celebrate our love for God
In my own fam-i-ly.
Parents, brother, sister, too,
Grandma, grandpa
I love you.
I'm so glad to be a part
Of my own fam-i-ly.

You may repeat the song without the *CD,* if desired. When you've finished singing, say: **Do you know that we're all members of one great, big, huge family? It's the family of God! Isn't it fun to celebrate together as a family? What are some ways we can celebrate God's love?** (We can be nice to each other; we can give presents to each other.)

**Families help each other and celebrate together. Now let's finish decorating our party table so we can celebrate together. Bop your balloons over to the table and tape them at your place.**

When children finish, say: **Doesn't our party table look nice? I wonder if our friend Pockets would like to join our celebration.**

 **The Point**

Practicing the Point

Pockets Plans a Party (up to 5 minutes)

Have children sit in a circle near the decorated table. Take out Pockets the Kangaroo and the bag of balloons. Make sure there are enough balloons for each child to have one. When you finish the script, put Pockets and the balloons out of sight.

Pockets Plans a Party

PUPPET SCRIPT

Pockets: *(Enters humming the "Wedding March.")* Hi, everyone! I bet you don't know what song I'm humming.

Teacher: It's the "Wedding March," isn't it?

Pockets: Yes... but I bet you don't know why I'm humming it.

Teacher: *(Very surprised.)* Are you getting married, Pockets?

Pockets: *(Putting her paw over her face in embarrassment)* Nooooo, I'm not getting married! I'm just a little kangaroo!

Teacher: Oh, that's right. Well, is it because we heard how Ruth and Boaz got married in the Bible story?

Pockets: They got married? My mommy and daddy got married, too. A long time ago! That's why we're having a party. Tomorrow is my mommy and daddy's anniversary party.

Teacher: That's wonderful, Pockets! What are you planning to do?

Pockets: Grandma made a big, beau-ti-ful cake and we invited our whole family to come. It's been so much fun and now we're gonna make lots of decorations.

Teacher: What are you going to make?

Pockets: We-ell *(scratching her head)*...I'm not sure. Can you help me think of something?

Teacher: We decorated with balloons to celebrate the wedding of Ruth and Boaz. We'd be glad to share some of our balloons. Children, let's give Pockets a balloon and tell her why families celebrate together.
(Have children hand Pockets a balloon from the bag. Encourage them to tell Pockets that celebrating good times shows love for our families.)

Pockets: Wow, thanks! Grandma loves balloons! My cousins can help blow them up. And Grandpa can help hang them! It'll be fun!

Teacher: Isn't it great that ● families help each other and celebrate together?

Pockets: It sure is! Thanks for the balloons. I'm going right over to Grandma's to start celebrating with my family. 'Bye everyone!
(Have children say goodbye to Pockets.)

 **The Point**

Families help each other.

TODAY I LEARNED...

We believe that Christian education extends beyond the classroom into the home. Photocopy the "Today I Learned..." handout (p. 66) for this week and send it home with your children. Encourage parents to use the handout to plan meaningful family activities to reinforce this week's topic. Follow up the "Today I Learned..." activities next week by asking children what their families did.

Closing

Party Time (up to 5 minutes)

Set the cupcakes and napkins on the party table.

Say: **Today we learned that ✏ families help each other and celebrate together. As members of God's family, let's celebrate the wedding of Ruth and Boaz by sharing the cupcakes we decorated!**

Let children take turns serving each other. As they offer each other a cupcake, have them say, "You're part of God's family." Then say: **We've been learning that ✏ families help each other and celebrate together. I'm so glad God made families and that we're all part of God's great big family. Let's pray.**

Pray: **Dear God, thank you for families and for the good times that we can celebrate. In Jesus' name we pray, amen.**

After children have enjoyed their treats, have them throw away their napkins and clean up. Remind them to take home their wedding-bell bags and to tell their families the story of Ruth and Boaz's wedding.

✏ **The Point**

✏ **The Point**

Families help each other.

For Extra Time

If you have a long class time or want to add additional elements to your lesson, try one of the following activities.

LIVELY LEARNING: Listening Center

For a fun review of this module's Bible stories, invite children to listen to the entire *Bible Big Book* story with the *CD*. Choose two children to hold the Big Book and turn the pages at the chimes. Help children begin at page 1. Listen and help them turn the pages at the appropriate times. The entire story is track 8 on the *CD*.

● **The Point**

MAKE TO TAKE: Instant Party!

Help children make an instant party to share. Set out colorful tissue paper, candies, and tape. Have children roll up the candies in the tissue paper, twist the ends, and tape them closed. Help them tie each tissue paper tube to an inflated balloon. As children work, ask who they're going to share their instant party with, and remind them that ● families help each other and celebrate together.

TREAT TO EAT: Graham-Cracker Crush

For each child, set out a plastic spoon, a 5-ounce cup of vanilla yogurt, a piece of wax paper, and half a graham cracker. Direct each child to fold the cracker inside the wax paper and crush it with the spoon. (Remind children that grain is crushed to make flour.) Have children sprinkle their cracker crumbs on top of their yogurt. As children make their treats, talk about special foods they enjoy during family celebrations. Remind them that ● families help each other and celebrate together.

● **The Point**

STORY PICTURE: Ruth and Boaz Marry

Give each child a photocopy of the "Today I Learned..." handout from page 66. Cover a table with newsprint. Set out glue, white tissue paper, paintbrushes or cotton swabs, and a small bowl of sugar. Let children glue small pieces of tissue paper on Ruth's dress. Then have them spread a thin layer of glue on the cakes and sprinkle them with sugar. As children work, talk about the happy times families celebrate together.

Families help each other.

Wedding Bells

Photocopy this handout. Cut out the bells.

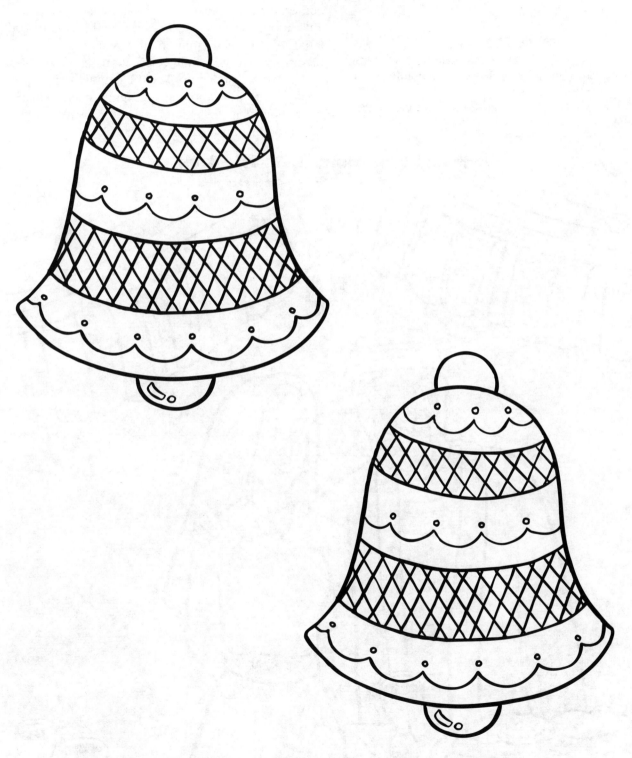

Families help each other.

TODAY I LEARNED...

The Point ✏ Families help each other and celebrate together.

Today your child learned that families help each other and celebrate together. Children learned that Ruth and Boaz got married. They talked about the importance of families celebrating the good things God gives them.

Verse to Learn

"As for me and my household, we will serve the Lord" (Joshua 24:15b).

Ask Me...

● How did Ruth and Boaz celebrate their wedding?
● How can you help your family celebrate good times?
● What are some ways our family can celebrate God's love?

Family Fun

● Celebrate God's love for your family with a Togetherness Night. Play favorite family games together. Talk about ways that God has shown his love in your family. Have each family member draw a picture of his or her favorite family celebration.

● Have a Celebration Week! Each night enjoy a favorite food. Talk about good things from God that your family can celebrate every day, such as your health, your house, or family pet.

Ruth and Boaz Marry (Ruth 3:1–4:16)

LESSON 4

Elijah

Ahab, the seventh king of Israel, did more to lead his nation into sin and idolatry than any king who had come before him. Ahab and his wife, Jezebel, brazenly led God's people into immoral practices and Baal worship. Enter God's prophet Elijah, who stood toe to toe with Ahab and pronounced God's judgment on Israel—a severe drought. Because Baal was the pagan god of fertility and rain, this punishment was particularly fitting. After years of drought had taken their toll, Elijah challenged the prophets of Baal to get their god to light a fire under an altar—but the false god fizzled. And in the fiery finale, God proved that he's the *only* true God.

It's important for kindergartners to understand that there's only one true God, who's all-powerful and can't be imitated. Kindergartners are well aware of name brand labels. From tennis shoes to bicycles, most young children (as well as adults!) will choose the "real thing" over a cheap imitation. Use the lessons in this module to teach children that the powerful God we serve is the <u>real</u> thing.

Four Lessons on Elijah

	Page	Point	Bible Basis
Lesson 5 **God Is Powerful**	73	Elijah knew that *God is powerful.*	1 Kings 17:1-24; 18:15-16
Lesson 6 **The One and Only**	87	*God is powerful, and he's the only true God.*	1 Kings 18:16-21
Lesson 7 **The Power of Prayer**	99	*God is powerful and answers our prayers.*	1 Kings 18:22-38
Lesson 8 **Praise Him! Praise Him!**	111	*God is powerful, and we can praise him.*	1 Kings 18:39

Time Stretchers

Power Leap

Tape two 3-foot pieces of masking tape to the floor a foot apart. Color one strip red and designate it as the starting line. Place the *power stamp and ink pad* from the Learning Lab beside the opposite line.

Hand each child a 3×5 card. Challenge children to put all their power into making mighty leaps! Let them leap from the starting line to the other piece of tape and shout out, "God is powerful!" Then use the *power stamp* to stamp their cards. When everyone's jumped, move the red tape a few inches farther from the other piece of tape.

After children are "leaped out," talk about the fact that God's power doesn't run out. Encourage children to use their stamped cards as special bookmarks that will remind them of God's power.

Oh, Elijah!

Give children a chance to echo the joy of knowing that God is powerful. Lead them in singing "Oh, Elijah!" to the tune of "Frère Jacques." This song does not appear on the *CD.* Sing each line to the children, then have them echo each line back to you.

Oh, Elijah! Oh, Elijah! *(Hands to mouth as if calling someone.)*
Prophet of God. Prophet of God. *(Point upward.)*
Elijah knew God's power. Elijah knew God's power. *(Make muscles with your arms.)*
Yes he did! Yes he did! *(Nod your head.)*

Oh, Elijah! Oh, Elijah! *(Make calling motions.)*
Pray to God. Pray to God. *(Fold your hands.)*
Start the fire burning. Start the fire burning. *(Rub your hands back and forth quickly.)*
Praise the Lord! Praise the Lord! *(Put your arms in the air.)*

On the Go

You'll enjoy this simple game any time you want to help kids work out the wiggles.

Choose three children to give the class traveling directions. Have the three direction-givers stand facing the rest of the class. One child tells the class <u>where</u> they'll travel, such as to the door or bulletin board. Another child tells <u>how</u> to get there, such as hopping or crawling. The third child tells <u>who's</u> traveling, such as kids wearing tennis shoes or the color blue. When you say "go," have the direction-givers tell what to do, then have the other children follow the directions. For the next round, choose other children to give three new directions.

As you play, explain that God sent Elijah to many places: to see King Ahab, to a river bank, to the widow's house, and back to Ahab. Elijah followed God's directions because he knew that God is powerful and that he's in charge of all we do.

Remembering God's Word

Each four- or five-week module focuses on a key Bible verse. The key verse for this module is "Great is our Lord and mighty in power; his understanding has no limit" (Psalm 147:5).

This module's key verse will help teach children that God is the one and only true God. Have fun using these ideas any time during the lessons on Elijah.

Pop-Ups

Lead children in singing "Great is Our Lord" to the tune of "Ten Little Indians." Sing the song without the *CD*. Have children sit on the floor and tell them to quickly stand up whenever they sing the word "Lord," then quickly sit down again. For real excitement, sing the song faster each time.

> **Great is our Lord and mighty in power.**
> **Great is our Lord and mighty in power.**
> **Great is our Lord and mighty in power.**
> **Great is our Lord!**
>
> **His understanding has no limit.**
> **His understanding has no limit.**
> **His understanding has no limit.**
> **Great is our Lord!**

Build a Verse

Gather children in a group. Repeat the key verse and tell children that they'll hear a story about God's great power. Explain that God is all-powerful and that we want to praise him for his might. Point out that in the Bible story, Elijah built a stone altar for God to show his great power to people in a wicked kingdom.

Tell children that they'll build a pretend altar while they say the words to the key verse. Choose a child to say the first word in the verse, then choose something from the classroom to build with, such as a chair, book, or wastebasket. Have that child lay the item on the floor. Then have a second child say the next word and place another item next to or on top of the first. Continue until the entire verse has been repeated and the pretend altar is built. Repeat the activity if there's time.

Story Enhancements

Make Bible stories come alive in your classroom by bringing in Bible costumes, setting out sensory items that fit with the story, or creating exciting bulletin boards to stimulate interest. When children learn with their five senses as well as their minds, lessons come alive and children remember them. Each week bring in one or more of the following items to help involve and motivate children in the Bible lessons they'll be learning. These ideas will get you started.

Module Bulletin Board Idea

Create a bulletin board to last for the entire module by allowing children to add different figures each week. Before Lesson 5, cover a bulletin board or section of the wall with green paper for the ground, brown paper for the hills, and blue paper for the sky. Cut a winding blue construction paper river and tape it across the hills on one side of the bulletin board. Draw and cut out a picture of Elijah. Pin the figure of Elijah beside the stream so it can be moved each week. Use the following directions for the bulletin board each week.

Lesson 5

● Bring in a variety of magnets and objects such as paper clips, erasers, nails, and pencils. Invite children to explore magnetic power and to try to pick up different items using various magnets. Point out that even though magnets seem strong, they're nothing compared to God's power. Remind children that nothing and no one is as powerful as God.

● Bring in olive oil, flour, and bread to taste. Tell children that people used oil and flour to make bread in Bible days, and if they ran out of either ingredient, they went hungry. Hand each child a piece of wheat bread to taste, while you explain that today's Bible story is about a time God's power kept a woman's oil and flour from running out.

● For the bulletin board, have children make ravens by gluing small paper triangles and circles to black craft feathers for beaks and eyes. Each time children tape a raven near Elijah, have them repeat the key verse or The Point for Lesson 5.

Lesson 6

● Bring in a clean spray bottle filled with water. Let children take turns giving their own hands or faces a spritz of water. Ask children questions such as "Whose power controls the rain and weather?" and "Who's the only one who can start and stop the rain?" Tell children that in today's story they'll hear about a time that God stopped the rain.

● Bring in an assortment of hats or other career-related accessories such as a baseball cap, a fireman's hat, a briefcase, and a paper crown. As children model those items, talk about the job each item represents and the importance of each job. Ask children if they think one job is more important or powerful than another. Point out that God is more powerful than anyone—even kings and queens and presidents.

● For the bulletin board, hand each child a sheet of newsprint or brown construction paper. Have children crumple the papers and tape them to the bulletin board to create a paper altar. As children place each "stone," have them repeat the key verse or The Point for Lesson 6.

Lesson 7

● Bring in stones, twigs, and a bowl of water. As you pass the items to the children, ask which of the items would burn if set on fire. Tell them they'll hear an exciting Bible story today about a time God's power burned wood, water, meat, and even stone!

● Bring in a candle and matches. Ask children how the candle could be lit. Point out that <u>God</u> doesn't need matches to light things—God's power can do anything. Tell children that in today's Bible story God miraculously melted stone and showed his power to many people. Light the candle and have children simultaneously say, "God is powerful!" Then blow out the candle.

● Bring in an assortment of rocks and stones. Invite children to stack the stones in a neat arrangement. Talk about how men in Bible days built altars for worship. Mention that in today's Bible story they'll hear how Elijah built an altar to God using 12 large stones. If there's time, do the "Build a Verse" activity from Remembering God's Word.

● For this lesson's bulletin board addition, have children cut flames from red, orange, and yellow construction paper. As they tape their flames above the altar, encourage them to repeat The Point for Lesson 7.

Lesson 8

● Bring in a cookie sheet containing burned newspaper ashes or ashes from a charcoal grill. Provide a damp washcloth for children to wipe their hands on. Let children touch the delicate ashes and talk about how they feel. Tell children that when the people in the Bible story saw God's power burn stone, wood, and water to ashes, they knew he was God.

✔ "Glowworms" or "snakes" left from Fourth of July celebrations, if they're legal in your state, make wonderful story enhancements for this lesson. Simply place a board outside and position children a foot away. Lay one or two glowworms on the board. Light the glowworms with a match and watch as they make delightful, wiggly ashes. When the ashes are cool, allow children to pick up the delicate ashes.

● Before class, write "God is powerful" on a sheet of paper, then tape it under the bulletin board. Bring in a box of alphabet cereal and let children work together to find letters in the sentence. Then have them use craft glue to attach the letters to the bulletin board as a title. Be sure to let children nibble some cereal as they work.

God Is Powerful

The Point

✏ Elijah knew that God is powerful.

The Bible Basis

1 Kings 17:1-24; 18:15-16. Elijah delivered God's punishment on an evil land.

King Ahab, who ruled Israel, was more wicked than any king before him. Pagan worship and heathen rituals finally caused God's anger to rise against Ahab's kingdom. Elijah confronted the wicked king and declared that God would send a searing drought across the land. After delivering his message to the defiant king, Elijah fled to the protective cover of a riverbank where God sent ravens to feed him. When the stream went dry, God sent Elijah to live in the house of a widow and her son. God miraculously confirmed his power by never allowing the starving widow's supply of flour and oil to be used up during the drought.

Kindergartners are fascinated by power. They love to watch earthmovers, rocket launches, and big diesel trucks. Television constantly bombards kids with super heroes, as each "super-slick lizard" or "mighty muscleman" is more powerful than the last. It's vitally important for young children to realize that these aren't real and that there isn't anyone or anything as powerful as <u>God.</u> Use this lesson to teach children that the only <u>real</u> super hero is the awesome and powerful God we serve!

Getting the Point

✏ **Elijah knew that God is powerful.**

It's important to say The Point just as it's written in each activity. Repeating The Point over and over will help the children remember it and apply it to their lives.

Children will
● explore the concept of power,
● discover that God is more powerful than anyone or anything,
● help Pockets learn that God is all-powerful, and
● learn that our powerful God helps us when we obey him.

✏ **The Point**

This Lesson at a Glance

Before the lesson, collect the necessary items for the activities you plan to use. Refer to the Classroom Supplies and Learning Lab Supplies columns to determine what you'll need. Remember to make photocopies of the "Today I Learned…" handout (p. 86) to send home with your children.

Section	Minutes	What Children Will Do	Classroom Supplies	Learning Lab Supplies
Welcome Time	up to 5	**Welcome!**—Receive name tags and be greeted by the teacher.	"Family Name Tags" handouts (p. 29), markers, pins or tape	
Let's Get Started Direct children to one or more of the Let's Get Started activities until everyone arrives.	up to 10	**Option 1: Barbelloons**—Make pretend barbells and do "exercises."	Balloons, plastic drinking straws, tape, black markers	
	up to 10	**Option 2: Story Pals**—Make story-character headbands to wear in Bible-Story Time.	"Story Pals" handouts (p. 85), glue sticks, scissors, markers, paper strips, yarn	
	up to 10	**Option 3: Power Prints**—Stamp pictures and learn that God's power never runs out.	Paper	Power stamp and ink pad
Pick-Up Song	up to 5	**We Will Pick Up**—Sing a song as they pick up toys and gather for Bible-Story Time.	CD player	CD: "We Will Pick Up" (track 2)
Bible-Story Time	up to 5	**Setting the Stage**—Explore the power of magnets and learn that God is more powerful than anything.	Magnets; a cookie sheet; assorted objects such as paper clips, erasers, nails, and pencils	
	up to 5	**Bible Song and Prayer Time**—Sing a song, bring out the Bible, and pray together.	Bible, construction paper, scissors, basket or box, CD player	CD: "God's Book" (track 3), power stamp and ink pad
	up to 10	**Hear the Bible Story**—Help tell the story of how God's power protected Elijah.	Bible, crackers, basket, story headbands from Option 2	Bible Big Book: Elijah & the Big Showdown (pp. 1-3)
	up to 10	**Do the Bible Story**—Play a fun game and learn that no one is as powerful as God.	Paper clips, magnets from "Setting the Stage"	
Practicing the Point	up to 5	**Super-Roo!**—Teach Pockets that only God has superpowers.	Pockets the Kangaroo, paper towel or scarf, tape, scissors, paper	
Closing	up to 5	**Powerful Praise**—Sing a lively song of praise, then say a prayer.	CD player	CD: "Shout With Joy" (track 9)
For Extra Time		For extra-time ideas and supplies, see page 84.		

God is powerful.

Welcome Time

Welcome! (up to 5 minutes)

- Bend down and make eye contact with children as they arrive.
- Greet each child individually with an enthusiastic smile.
- Thank each child for coming to class today.
- Say: **Today we're going to learn ✏️Elijah knew that God is powerful.**
- Hand out the "Family" name tags children made in Lesson 1 and help them attach the name tags to their clothing. If some of the name tags were damaged or if some of the children weren't in class that week, have them make new name tags using the photocopiable patterns on page 29.
- Direct children to the Let's Get Started activities you've set up.

⬤ **The Point**

Let's Get Started

Set up one or more of the following activities for children to do as they arrive. After you greet each child, invite him or her to choose an activity.

Circulate among the children to offer help as needed and direct children's conversation toward today's lesson. Ask questions such as "Who is more powerful than anyone or anything?" and "How does God's power help us?"

☐ Option 1: Barbelloons (up to 10 minutes)

Before class, blow up and tie two balloons for each child. Try to make all the balloons the same size.

Set out plastic drinking straws, tape, and black markers. Invite children to make sets of barbells by slipping the ends of the balloons over the ends of drinking straws and taping them in place. Help children write numbers on the balloons representing the weight of their "barbelloons," such as 100 or 200 pounds. As children work, explain that people lift barbells to make them powerful and strong. Mention that many things seem powerful, but that God is more powerful than anyone or anything. Tell children they'll hear an exciting Bible story about a man named Elijah and how ✏️Elijah knew that God is powerful.

When you're finished, encourage children to exercise by lifting their barbelloons with their hands, chins, or even their toes.

⬤ **The Point**

☐ Option 2: Story Pals (up to 10 minutes)

Before class, photocopy the "Story Pals" handout from page 85. Each child will need one character face from the handout. Also cut a construction paper strip for each child to use as a headband.

Set out paper strips, glue sticks, the character faces, markers, scissors, and yarn. Let each child choose a character's face to decorate with markers and yarn. Then have children cut out the patterns and glue them to their paper strips. Then have children glue the ends of their strips together to make headbands. While children make their headbands, ask questions such as "When is a time God's power helped you?" and "Why does God use his power to help us?" Tell children they'll hear a Bible story today about a time God used his power in an amazing way.

Be sure children's names are on the backs of the headbands, then set the headbands aside to use later.

☐ OPTION 3: Power Prints (up to 10 minutes)

Set out paper and the *power stamp and ink pad* found in the Learning Lab. As children arrive, invite them to make "power prints" by stamping the *power stamp* on paper. Have them count how many times they can make a print without re-inking the stamper. Make comments such as "Notice how the ink gets weak and runs out? I'm glad God's power doesn't!" and "God's power lasts forever." Mention that today's Bible story is about God's power, and how a man named Elijah used that power to teach people that there's only one true God.

Note:
If the ink pad is dry, moisten it with three to five drops of water.

✔ If you have a large class, you may also want to use the *family stamp* from Module 1 and other rubber stamps from previous quarters of Group's Hands-On Bible Curriculum™.

When everyone has arrived and you're ready to move on to the Bible-Story Time, encourage the children to finish what they're doing and get ready to clean up.

Pick-Up Song

We Will Pick Up (up to 5 minutes)

Lead children in singing "We Will Pick Up" (track 2) with the *CD* to the tune of "London Bridge." Encourage children to sing along as they help clean up the room.

If you want to include the names of all the children in your class, sing the song without the *CD* and repeat the naming section. If you choose to use the *CD,* vary the names you use each week.

Sing

We will pick up all our toys,
All our toys, all our toys.
We will pick up all our toys
And put them all away.

I see (name) picking up,
Picking up, picking up.
I see (name) picking up
And putting toys away.

(Repeat.)

God is powerful.

Bible-Story Time

Setting the Stage (up to 5 minutes)

Tell the children you'll clap your hands to get their attention. Explain that when you clap your hands, the children are to stop what they're doing, raise their hands, and focus on you. Practice this signal a few times. Encourage children to respond quickly so you'll have time for all the fun activities you've planned.

Before class, place paper clips, small erasers, pencils, nails, and other magnetic and nonmagnetic objects on a cookie sheet. Collect a variety of magnets including refrigerator magnets, bar magnets, and horseshoe magnets.

Sit in a circle and place the cookie sheet and magnets in the center. Lift up a paper clip using a magnet. Ask:

● **How did I pick up the paper clip without touching it?** (With a magnet; the magnet's power picked it up.)

Say: **Magnets have power to pick up different things. See if you can find things to lift with these magnets.** Encourage children to try each different magnet with every item on the cookie sheet. When everyone's had a few turns, ask:

● **What things did the magnets pick up?** (Paper clips; nails; the cookie sheet.)

● **Why didn't the magnets lift the other items?** (The things weren't made of metal; the magnet didn't work on them.)

Say: **Magnets seem powerful when they pick things up, but magnets can't lift everything—they have limited power. Do you know someone whose power has no limits at all?** Lead children to suggest that God's powers aren't limited.

Say: **God is powerful. And his power never gets weak or runs out. God is more powerful than anyone or anything—even the strongest magnet. In our Bible story today, we'll meet a man whose name is Elijah. Let's listen to our story and find out why ◗ Elijah knew that God is powerful.**

If there's time, let children go around the room in pairs and see what else the magnets pick up.

Bible Song and Prayer Time (up to 5 minutes)

Before class, make surprise cards for this activity by cutting construction paper into 2×6-inch slips. Prepare a surprise card for each child, plus a few extras for visitors. Fold the cards in half, then stamp the *power stamp* inside one of the surprise cards. Mark 1 Kings 17:1-24; 18:15-16 in the Bible you'll be using.

Have children sit in a circle. Say: **Now it's time to choose a Bible person to bring me the Bible marked with today's Bible story. As we sing our Bible song, I'll pass out the surprise cards. Don't look inside your card until the song is over.**

Lead children in singing "God's Book" (track 3) with the *CD* to the tune of "Old MacDonald Had a Farm." As you sing, pass out the folded surprise cards. If you want to include the names of all the children in your class, sing the song without the *CD* and repeat the naming section. If you choose to use the *CD*, vary the names you use each week.

● **The Point**

Sing

Now it's time to read God's Book
And hear a Bible story.
It's fun to be here with my
    friends
And hear a Bible story.
	Now it's time to read God's Book
	And hear a Bible story.
	It's fun to be here with my
	    friends
	And hear a Bible story.

(Name)'s **here.** (Name)'s **here.** **Here is** (name). **Here is** (name). Now it's time to read God's Book And hear a Bible story.	(Name)'s **here.** (Name)'s **here.** **Here is** (name). **Here is** (name). Now it's time to read God's Book And hear a Bible story.

After the song, say: **You may look inside your surprise cards. The person who has the *power stamp* stamped inside his or her card will be our Bible person for today.**

Identify the Bible person, then have the rest of the children clap for him or her. Ask the Bible person to bring you the Bible. Help the Bible person open the Bible to the marked place and show children where your story comes from. Then have the Bible person sit down.

Say: (Name) **was our special Bible person today. Each week, we'll have only one special Bible person, but each one of you is a special part of our**

🔹 **The Point**

class! Today we're all learning that 🔹 Elijah knew that God is powerful.

Let's say a special prayer now and ask God to help us learn about his power. I'll pass around this basket. When the basket comes to you, put your surprise card in it and say, "God, help us learn that you're powerful."

Pass around the basket or box. When you've collected everyone's surprise card, set the basket aside and pick up the Bible. Lead children in this prayer: **God, thank you for the Bible and all the stories in it. Teach us today**

🔹 **The Point**

that 🔹 Elijah knew that you are powerful. Amen.

Hear the Bible Story (up to 10 minutes)

Before class, fill a basket with small crackers.

Bring out the *Bible Big Book: Elijah & the Big Showdown.* Set the basket containing crackers at one end of the room. Have children gather around and ask:

● **Who can tell about a time you told an important message?**

Allow time for children to tell their experiences. Say: **The Bible tells us about different people who told important messages from God. These people were called prophets. God's prophets told people when God was angry or when God wanted them to do things. Elijah was one of God's**

🔹 **The Point**

prophets, and Elijah knew something very important. 🔹 Elijah knew that God is powerful.

Hold up your Bible. **Our Bible story comes from the book of 1 Kings in the Bible.** Hold up the *Bible Big Book: Elijah & the Big Showdown.* **Our Big Book shows us pictures of the Bible story. You can help me tell the story with the story-character headbands you made.** Hand out the

God is powerful.

story-character headbands children made in Option 2. If some of the children chose not to do this option, they may be ravens. Say: **Hold your headbands up.** Pause. **Oh! I see lots of Elijahs and widows and nasty kings in our room! All Elijahs, wave your hands. Good. All widows, hop up and down. And nasty kings, shake your fists and grumble. Good for you. The rest of you are big black birds called ravens. Flap your wings, ravens.** Pause for children without headbands to respond.

Say: **Listen to the story carefully. If I say the name of your story headband, hold the headband on your head. If I say the word "raven," the ravens will fly to the basket and take one cracker to each person in the class and keep one for themselves. Save your crackers until I tell you to eat them.**

Open the *Bible Big Book* so children see page 1. Read the following story and pause while children respond to the underlined words.

Our God is strong and powerful. In fact, there isn't anyone or anything in the whole world that's as powerful as God. But once there was a wicked <u>king</u> who didn't believe in God. Listen to what happened when God's prophet <u>Elijah</u> challenged the wicked <u>king</u> to a showdown.

Long ago there lived a wicked <u>king</u> named Ahab. <u>King</u> Ahab and his evil wife, Queen Jezebel, ruled God's people in the nation of Israel. The <u>king</u> and queen didn't love God. Instead, they worshiped idols made of wood and stone. Soon the people of Israel started worshiping idols, too.

God decided to punish wicked <u>King</u> Ahab. God sent the prophet <u>Elijah</u> to tell the evil <u>king</u> what would happen.

"Instead of worshiping the God of Israel, you've worshiped idols made of wood and stone," <u>Elijah</u> proclaimed. "Now here is what will happen. The God I serve has said there will be no rain in this land for years to come. That is your punishment."

When <u>King</u> Ahab heard this news, he roared with fury. God told <u>Elijah</u> to go hide by a brook where he would be safe from the angry <u>king</u>.

Just as <u>Elijah</u> said, not a drop of rain fell in Ahab's kingdom. Days turned into weeks and weeks into months, but there was still no rain. Not one little drop. The grass dried up. Plants wilted away. Trees turned brown in the glaring sun. Since crops couldn't grow, there wasn't enough food. <u>King</u> Ahab was learning that our God is powerful.

Turn the page and show children the picture on pages 2 and 3. Read: **All during the drought, <u>Elijah</u> stayed by the brook and God took care of him there. Every morning and evening, God sent <u>ravens</u> carrying bread and meat for <u>Elijah</u> to eat.**

As the months went by, the little stream began to dry up. So God told <u>Elijah</u> to leave his hiding place and go to the town of Zarephath where he would find a <u>woman</u> who would give him food and a place to stay.

So <u>Elijah</u> traveled to Zarephath. When he got to the city gate, he found a <u>woman</u> gathering sticks.

"Would you give me a drink of water and a piece of bread?" <u>Elijah</u> asked.

"We have only a little flour and oil to bake bread," the <u>woman</u> replied.

"Don't worry," said <u>Elijah</u>. "God will not let you run out of flour and oil."

So the <u>woman</u> made bread and shared it with <u>Elijah</u>. And guess what happened—she never ran out of flour and oil! Whenever she poured flour

God is powerful.

and oil from her jars, God filled them back up again. It was a miracle!

Close the *Bible Big Book*. Ask:

● **Why did God stop the rain in King Ahab's land?** (Because Ahab and his people didn't believe in God and his power; because King Ahab and the people worshiped idols.)

● **How did Elijah obey God?** (He warned King Ahab; he went to hide where God told him; he went to find the woman.)

● **How did God's power take care of Elijah?** (By sending him food; by telling Elijah where it was safe to hide.)

● **Why do you think God used his power to help Elijah?** (Because God loved Elijah; because God wanted people to know about his power; because God wanted to help the woman and her son; because Elijah obeyed God.)

Say: **Elijah obeyed God and trusted in his power. When we obey God and trust in his power, then God works through us to help others, just like Elijah helped the widow and her son.**

● **The Point**

● **Elijah knew that God is powerful and he wanted others to know that, too. Even when Elijah was in danger from the angry king, Elijah trusted in God's power to help him. We can trust in God's power, too. Now turn to the person on your right and feed him or her a cracker, like the ravens fed Elijah. Then tell that person, "God is powerful."** Be sure each child receives a cracker.

Do the Bible Story (up to 10 minutes)

Place a large pile of paper clips at one end of the room. Form two lines at the opposite end of the room and hand the first child in each line a magnet. Make sure the magnets are similar in size.

● **The Point**

Say: **It's important that ● Elijah knew that God is powerful, and it's important for us to remember that, too. Let's play an exciting game to remind us of God's awesome power. When I clap my hands, the first person in each line will hop to the pile of paper clips. Use your magnet to pick up some paper clips, then hop back to your line. Scoop the paper clips off your magnet then hand the magnet to the next person in line so he or she can have a turn. We'll see who has the biggest pile when we're done.**

Continue the game until each child's had a turn to pick up paper clips.

✔ If you have an unusually large number of children, limit the number of paper clips they may pick up to one or two.

Gather the children together. Ask:

● **How did the magnets' power help you gather paper clips?** (The magnets lifted the paper clips up; the magnets held the paper clips and kept them from falling.)

● **Could you see the magnets' power? Then how did you know the power was there?** (I couldn't see the power, but I saw what it does; I saw the paper clips move.)

● **How is this like God's power?** (We can see God's power by what he does; we know about God's power because he uses it to help people.)

God is powerful.

Say: **Even though we may not be able to see God's power, we can see what God's power does.**

● **How did God's power help Elijah?** (God sent the ravens to feed Elijah; God made sure that the flour and oil never ran out.)

Say: **Elijah could see what God's power did, too, and that's why Elijah knew that God is powerful.**

● **How does God's power help us?** (God's power helps us have faith; it helps us be kind to others; his power helps us be brave if we're scared; he makes sure I have food and clothes.)

Say: **There's nothing as awesome as our powerful God. No one and nothing is as powerful as he is. Isn't that neat? Let's see if Pockets knows who's the most powerful of all!**

 **The Point**

Practicing the Point

Super-Roo! (up to 5 minutes)

Before class, fasten a paper towel or scarf like a cape around Pockets' neck. Make Pockets a small mask to wear by cutting a 2×6-inch strip of paper. Cut eye holes in the paper, then tape the mask to Pockets' face.

Bring out Pockets the Kangaroo and go through the following puppet script. When you finish the script, put Pockets away and out of sight.

Super-Roo!

PUPPET SCRIPT

Pockets: *(Hops all around as if she's flying. Pockets is excited and shouting.)* I can leap tall buildings in a single bound! I'm faster than a lightning bolt! I'm here and there—I'm every-where! I'm SUPER-ROO!

Teacher: Pockets, Pockets . . . *(patting her on the head to calm her down)*, what are you doing? And who is Super-Roo?

Pockets: Who is Super-Roo? I'm Super-Roo! *(Begins hopping again and pretends to fly.)* I'm Super-Roo and I'm the fastest, biggest, strongest, most powerful kangaroo in the world!

Teacher: It's fun to pretend that we're powerful and strong, isn't it?

Pockets: *(Indignantly)* Who's pretending? There's no one or nothing as strong as I am!

Teacher: Pockets, can you make the rain start?

Pockets: Welll . . . no.

Teacher: Can you make the rain stop?

Pockets: Uh . . . no, I guess not.

(Continued)

God is powerful.

Teacher: Can you fill up someone's flour jar with flour so it never runs out of flour for bread and cookies?

Pockets: No, I can't do that either. *(Shaking her head)* No one can do all those things!

Teacher: We heard a story today about someone who can do all those things and much, much more. Children, let's tell Pockets about our Bible story and what powerful things God did for Elijah.

(Have the children tell Pockets about the Bible story. Encourage them to tell how God kept Elijah safe and fed, and how God's power miraculously kept the widow's flour and oil jugs full. Lead children in repeating The Point.)

Pockets: Wow! God really is the most powerful of all! God can do anything!

Teacher: That's right, Pockets. Just as ⬤ Elijah knew that God is powerful, we know there isn't anyone or anything as powerful as our God.

Pockets: I'm glad that God is powerful and that he loves me. Do you think God would mind if I just pretend to be strong?

Teacher: I don't think he'd mind, Pockets. But always remember where real power comes from—it comes from God.

Pockets: *(Pretending to fly and chanting the following rhyme)*
I'm here! I'm there!
I'm big and strong and tall!
I may be strong for "Super-Roo,"
But God is strongest of all!

⬤ **The Point**

TODAY I LEARNED . . .

We believe that Christian education extends beyond the classroom into the home. Photocopy the "Today I Learned . . ." handout (p. 86) for this week and send it home with your children. Encourage parents to use the handout to plan meaningful family activities to reinforce this week's topic. Follow up the "Today I Learned . . ." activities next week by asking children what their families did.

⬤ **The Point**

Closing

Powerful Praise (up to 5 minutes)

Gather children in a circle. Say: **We've been learning today that ⬤ Elijah knew God that is powerful. We know that God is powerful, too, and that makes me want to sing for joy. Let's sing praises to our powerful God with a new song.**

God is powerful.

Lead children in singing "Shout With Joy" (track 9) with the *CD* to the tune of "Old MacDonald Had a Farm." Encourage children to clap their hands in time to the music and follow along with the actions in the song.

Sing

Clap your hands, now ev'ryone.
Shout to God with joy . . . JOY!
The Lord our God is powerful.
Shout to God with joy . . . JOY!

Clap your hands.
March around.
Jump up high.
Now bend down.
Clap your hands, now ev'ryone.
Shout to God with joy . . . JOY!

(Repeat.)

Turn off the CD player. Ask:
● **Who is more powerful than anyone or anything?** (God.)

Say: **Right! And we're thankful that we serve such a powerful God. Let's say a prayer and thank God for his awesome power.** Pray: **Dear God, thank you for being more powerful than anything or anybody. We know you love us and you use your power to help us. We love you, too. In Jesus' name, amen.**

God is powerful.

For Extra Time

If you have a long class time or want to add additional elements to your lesson, try one of the following activities.

LIVELY LEARNING: That's the Way to Obey

Gather children around you and give multiple directions for them to follow, such as "Walk to the table, pick up a pencil, then come back and sit down" or "Hop around the chair two times and say, "God Loves Me!" After you've given the directions, allow children time to obey. Give each child a turn to be the caller. Point out that Elijah obeyed God because ◑ Elijah knew that God is powerful. Tell children it's important to obey our powerful God, just as Elijah did.

◑ **The Point**

MAKE TO TAKE: Powerful Reminders

Before class purchase a self-sticking magnetic strip from a craft store. Cut a 1-inch segment of magnetic strip for each child. Leave the paper backing on the magnetic strip. Help children write the words "God is powerful!" on 3×5 cards.

Set out markers, glitter glue, and the pieces of magnetic strip. Encourage children to use markers and glitter glue to decorate the cards. Have children peel the paper backing from their magnetic strips and stick them to the backs of their cards. As children work, remind them that ◑ Elijah knew that God is powerful and that the magnets will remind them that God's power is greater than anyone or anything.

◑ **The Point**

TREAT TO EAT: Ravin' Ravens

Let your children make delicious "cookie ravens" to remind them how God used his power to send food to Elijah by ravens.

Set out plastic knives, peanut butter, chocolate chips, and two cheese slices. Hand each child a napkin and two chocolate sandwich cookies. Have children use the plastic knives to cut small triangular-shaped beaks from the cheese slices, and fasten the beaks to the cookies using peanut butter "glue." Then dab a bit of peanut butter on the top of each cookie and push two chocolate chips in the peanut butter for eyes.

As children enjoy eating their special ravens, encourage them to retell how and why God sent ravens to feed Elijah. Remind children that ◑ Elijah knew that God is powerful.

◑ **The Point**

STORY PICTURE: Bread From Heaven

Photocopy the "Today I Learned..." handout from page 86 for each child. Set out crayons, a small dish of cooking oil, and cotton swabs. Invite children to color their pictures. Then direct them to dip cotton swabs in the cooking oil and "paint" portions of their pictures. When they've finished, have children hold their pictures up to a light or a window. The oil will give the paper a stained-glass look. Blot off excess oil with a tissue. Wrap the pictures in wax paper to protect clothing from any oil.

God is powerful.

Story Pals

Photocopy this page. Cut out the faces then color them.

TODAY I LEARNED . . .

The Point ✏ Elijah knew that God is powerful.

Today your child learned that Elijah knew that God is powerful. Children learned that God can do miracles and is more powerful than anyone or anything. They also talked about how God uses his power to help them.

Verse to Learn

"Great is our Lord and mighty in power; his understanding has no limit" (Psalm 147:5).

Ask Me . . .

● What powerful things did God do to help Elijah?

● How can you trust God's power to help you?

● How can our family obey God like Elijah obeyed?

Family Fun

● Go on a "power" walk through the park. As you walk briskly, look for signs of God's great power. Take turns creating power sentences with your child such as "God's power is in the wind," "God's power is in the birds that fly," or "God's power is in the sunshine." Point out that God's power is everywhere—God has even given your hearts the power to beat quickly as you walk.

God's Power Helps Elijah and the Widow (1 Kings 17:1-24; 8:15-16)

The One and Only

The Point

✏ God is powerful, and he's the only true God.

The Bible Basis

1 Kings 18:16-21. Elijah challenges King Ahab to a showdown between Ahab's pagan god and the one true God.

After the brook where he had been hiding dried up, Elijah obeyed God and stayed with a widow and her son in the town of Zarephath. Safe, cared for, and hidden from King Ahab's wrath, Elijah awaited God's next directives concerning Israel's king. Finally God directed Elijah to search out the king and issue the ultimate challenge—a showdown of force between Ahab's pagan god and the one true God. Each side would build an altar and prepare a sacrifice, then they would pray for fire to consume the sacrifice. God's anger was set to burn against pagan idol worship and prove once and for all that the God of Israel is the only true God!

Even young children sometimes have false "gods" in their lives. They crave the latest toys, the best sports equipment, or the most trendy clothing. Children (and many adults!) may begin to serve physical things and lose sight of the truth that God alone deserves our allegiance. Use this lesson to teach children that there's only one true God and that God wants us to worship only him.

Another Scripture used in this lesson is Deuteronomy 5:6-9a.

Getting the Point

✏ **God is powerful, and he's the only true God.**

It's important to say The Point just as it's written in each activity. Repeating The Point over and over will help the children remember it and apply it to their lives.

Children will
- learn that there is only one real God,
- understand that God wants us to worship only him,
- help Pockets learn that our God is the true God, and
- realize the differences between real and fake things.

✏ **The Point**

God is powerful.

This Lesson at a Glance

Before the lesson, collect the necessary items for the activities you plan to use. Refer to the Classroom Supplies and Learning Lab Supplies columns to determine what you'll need. Remember to make photocopies of the "Today I Learned..." handout (p. 98) to send home with your children.

Section	Minutes	What Children Will Do	Classroom Supplies	Learning Lab Supplies
Welcome Time	up to 5	**Welcome!**—Receive name tags and be greeted by the teacher.	"Family Name Tags" handouts (p. 29), markers, pins or tape	
Let's Get Started Direct children to one or more of the Let's Get Started activities until everyone arrives.	up to 10	**Option 1: Carbon Copies**—Copy pictures and learn that there's only one original.	White paper, paper clips, carbon paper, pencils	
	up to 10	**Option 2: Phony Food?**—Create foods from modeling dough and talk about the differences between what's real and what's not.	Modeling dough, vinyl place mats	
	up to 10	**Option 3: One Name Game**—Play a spelling game and learn there's only one powerful name.	15 dried lima beans, fine-tip marker, lunch sack	
Pick-Up Song	up to 5	**We Will Pick Up**—Sing a song as they pick up toys and gather for Bible-Story Time.	CD player	CD: "We Will Pick Up" (track 2)
Bible-Story Time	up to 5	**Setting the Stage**—Explore the differences between real and fake rocks, then listen to what the Bible says about worshiping the real God.	Bible, small rocks, rock candy, lunch sack, hammer	
	up to 5	**Bible Song and Prayer Time**—Sing a song, bring out the Bible, and pray together.	Bible, construction paper, scissors, basket or box, CD player	CD: "God's Book" (track 3), power stamp and ink pad
	up to 10	**Hear the Bible Story**—Help their groups answer review questions, then listen to the challenge Elijah gave King Ahab in 1 Kings 18:16-21.	Bible, CD player	Bible Big Book: Elijah & the Big Showdown (pp. 1-4), CD: "Elijah & the Big Showdown" (track 10)
	up to 10	**Do the Bible Story**—Use their sense of smell to find real flowers.	Real flowers, silk flowers, vases, CD player	CD: "One True God" (track 11)
Practicing the Point	up to 5	**True Blue**—Help Pockets learn about the one true God.	Pockets the Kangaroo, a real flower from "Do the Bible Story"	
Closing	up to 5	**Real Thank You's**—Affirm each other and say a prayer.	Real flower	
For Extra Time		For extra-time ideas and supplies, see page 97.		

God is powerful.

Welcome Time

Welcome! (up to 5 minutes)

● Bend down and make eye contact with children as they arrive.

● Greet each child individually with an enthusiastic smile.

● Thank each child for coming to class today.

● Ask children about the discussion from last week's "Today I Learned..." handout. Ask questions such as "How did God's power help you last week?" and "How did you obey God last week as Elijah obeyed God?"

● Say: **Today we're going to learn that ◐ God is powerful, and he's the only true God.**

● Hand out the "Family" name tags children made in the first lesson and help them attach the name tags to their clothing. If some of the name tags were damaged or if some of the children weren't in class that week, have them make new name tags using the photocopiable patterns on page 29.

● Direct children to the Let's Get Started activities you've set up.

◐ **The Point**

Let's Get Started

Set up one or more of the following activities for children to do as they arrive. After you greet each child, invite him or her to choose an activity.

Circulate among the children to offer help as needed and direct children's conversation toward today's lesson. Ask questions such as "How do you know if something is real?" and "When's a time you were fooled by something that wasn't real?"

▢ OPTION 1: Carbon Copies (up to 10 minutes)

Before this activity, place a sheet of carbon paper between two sheets of white paper, carbon side down. Fasten the pages together with paper clips. Make one set of pages for each child. (Instead of preparing carbon paper sets, you may simply wish to let children visit the church office and make photocopies of their original drawings.)

Set out the carbon paper sets and pencils. As children arrive, invite them to draw a picture of something or someone real. Tell them to leave the paper clips in place. As they draw, ask questions such as "Which is better: something real or fake? Why?" and "How do you tell if something's real or fake?"

When children are finished, have them remove the paper clips and hand them to you. Encourage them to compare their original drawings with the copies. Point out that copies are like phonies; they aren't the real thing and may be different from the original. Explain that ◐ God is powerful, and he's the only true God—there are no copies. Mention that in today's Bible story they'll hear about a time when people thought that our powerful God wasn't the only God, but they soon found out the others were fakes. If there's time, have children color their "real" pictures using crayons.

◐ **The Point**

OPTION 2: Phony Food? (up to 10 minutes)

Set out modeling dough and vinyl place mats. As children arrive, invite them to make models of their favorite food items, such as pizza or hamburgers. As children work, ask questions such as "How do you know if food is real or phony?" and "Would you like to eat the food you're making? Why not?" Point out that just like modeling-dough apples are poor imitations of real apples, idols like King Ahab worshiped can't copy our true God. Explain that ⬤ God is powerful, and he's the only true God, and that no one or nothing can copy God's power.

● **The Point**

OPTION 3: One Name Game (up to 10 minutes)

Before class gather 15 dried lima beans. On five beans write the letter G. Write O on five beans and D on five beans. Place the beans in a lunch sack with the word "GOD" written on it.

Set the sack on the floor and invite children to play a spelling game with you. Show children God's name on the lunch sack. Take turns reaching into the sack and pulling out the beans. The first person to collect all the letters in God's name says, "God is powerful!"

Tell children that today they'll hear a story about a time Elijah wanted the people to know that there's only one God. Explain that God helped Elijah show everyone that ⬤ God is powerful, and he's the only true God.

● **The Point**

If there's time, play the game again with a different twist. Each time someone draws a letter, he or she says a word that describes God with that letter in it, such as "great" for the letter G, or "powerful" for the letter O.

✔ Keep the games you make handy for rainy days or a quick time stuffer. Decorate a storage box to hold your games so they're ready in a snap.

When everyone has arrived and you're ready to move on to the Bible-Story Time, encourage the children to finish what they're doing and get ready to clean up.

Pick-Up Song

We Will Pick Up (up to 5 minutes)

Lead children in singing "We Will Pick Up" (track 2) with the *CD* to the tune of "London Bridge." Encourage children to sing along as they help clean up the room.

If you want to include the names of all the children in your class, sing the song without the *CD* and repeat the naming section. If you choose to use the *CD,* vary the names you use each week.

God is powerful.

Sing

We will pick up all our toys,
All our toys, all our toys.
We will pick up all our toys
And put them all away.

I see (name) picking up,
Picking up, picking up.
I see (name) picking up
And putting toys away.

(Repeat.)

Bible-Story Time

Setting the Stage (up to 5 minutes)

Tell the children you'll clap your hands to get their attention. Explain that when you clap your hands, the children are to stop what they're doing, raise their hands, and focus on you. Practice this signal a few times. Encourage children to respond quickly so you'll have time for all the fun activities you've planned.

Before class, place a few real rocks and a few pieces of rock candy or hard candy in a paper bag. Save extra rock candy for children to taste later.

Gather children in a circle. Say: **Let's see if you can tell what I have in this bag.** Invite children to reach into the bag and identify what they feel.

When everyone's had a turn, ask:

● **What's in the bag?** (Rocks; stones; something hard.)

● **Are they real or fake rocks? How do you know?** (They're real because they're hard; they're real because they feel rough; they're fake because they're too small for rocks.)

Say: **Sometimes it's hard to tell something real from something fake.** Pull the rocks and rock candy from the bag. Set them on the paper sack and allow each child to lightly tap the real and fake rocks with a hammer. Ask:

● **Can you tell which are the real rocks now? How?** (Yes, the real ones didn't crumble; the candy ones broke apart.)

Say: **Real rocks are strong and don't crumble when they're tapped. But candy isn't a rock, and it isn't strong like a rock, so when it is tapped, it falls apart. We can tell when something is real by what it does. We know our powerful God is real by what he does. In our Bible story today, some people worshiped fake gods. Just like fake rocks, the fake gods couldn't do what our real God can do. God wants us to know that there's only one true God. And God wants us to worship only him. Let's read what the Bible tells us about the true God.** Read Deuteronomy 5:6-9a from an easy-to-understand version of the Bible. Ask:

● **What does the Bible say about who God wants us to worship?** (That we're to worship only him; that there are no other gods.)

● **How do you think God would feel if we worshiped fake gods?** (He'd be mad; he'd be sad; he wouldn't like it at all.)

Say: **✐God is powerful, and he's the only true God. In our Bible story today, God became very angry at a king and his kingdom because they worshiped fake gods—and didn't worship the real God. Now let's enjoy**

● The Point

some real candy and enjoy listening to the Bible story. We'll find out more about our exciting, powerful God. Give each child a piece of fresh rock candy to eat.

Bible Song and Prayer Time (up to 5 minutes)

Before class, make surprise cards for this activity by cutting construction paper into 2×6-inch slips. Prepare a surprise card for each child, plus a few extras for visitors. Fold the cards in half, then stamp the *power stamp* inside one of the surprise cards. Mark 1 Kings 18:16-21 in the Bible you'll be using.

Have children sit in a circle. Say: **Now it's time to choose a Bible person to bring me the Bible marked with today's Bible story. As we sing our Bible song, I'll pass out the surprise cards. Don't look inside your card until the song is over.**

Lead children in singing "God's Book" (track 3) with the *CD* to the tune of "Old MacDonald Had a Farm." As you sing, pass out the folded surprise cards. If you want to include the names of all the children in your class, sing the song without the *CD* and repeat the naming section. If you choose to use the *CD*, vary the names you use each week.

Sing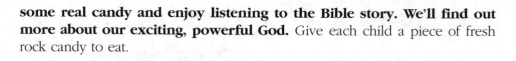

Now it's time to read God's Book	Now it's time to read God's Book
And hear a Bible story.	And hear a Bible story.
It's fun to be here with my friends	It's fun to be here with my friends
And hear a Bible story.	And hear a Bible story.
(Name)'s here.	(Name)'s here.
(Name)'s here.	(Name)'s here.
Here is (name).	Here is (name).
Here is (name).	Here is (name).
Now it's time to read God's Book	Now it's time to read God's Book
And hear a Bible story.	And hear a Bible story.

After the song, say: **You may look inside your surprise cards. The person who has power stamped inside his or her card will be our Bible person for today.**

Identify the Bible person, then have the rest of the children clap for him or her. Ask the Bible person to bring you the Bible. Help the Bible person open the Bible to the marked place and show children where your story comes from. Then have the Bible person sit down.

● **The Point**

Say: (Name) **was our special Bible person today. Each week, we'll have only one special Bible person, but each one of you is a special part of our class! Today we're all learning that ● God is powerful, and he's the only true God.**

Let's say a special prayer now and ask God to help us learn more about his power. I'll pass around this basket. When the basket comes to you, put your surprise card in it and say, "God, help us learn that you're the only true God."

Pass around the basket or box. When you've collected everyone's surprise card, set the basket aside and pick up the Bible. Lead children in this prayer:

God, thank you for the Bible and all the stories in it. Teach us today that  you are powerful, and you're the only true God. Amen.

Hear the Bible Story (up to 10 minutes)

Form three groups with the children. Say: **Before we listen to our exciting story, let's review what's happened so far to Elijah and wicked King Ahab. I'll ask story questions. Huddle with your group and decide on an answer. When your group has an answer, pop up and raise your hands. I'll let groups take turns answering questions. If the group I call on gives the right answer, clap your hands. If it's not the right answer, raise your hands again and I'll call on someone else.** Ask children the following story questions or make up some of your own.

● **Why was God angry with wicked King Ahab?** (Ahab worshiped fake gods; Ahab didn't love or obey God.)

● **What did Elijah say would happen?** (God would stop the rain; the land would be dried out.)

● **What's a prophet?** (A prophet tells messages from God; they tell if God is angry or glad and what God will do.)

● **Where did God hide Elijah? How did Elijah get food?** (He hid near a river; God sent food by ravens.)

● **When the river dried up, where did God send Elijah?** (To stay with a widow and her son; to Zarephath.)

● **What miracle did God perform to help the widow?** (He didn't let her run out of flour and oil.)

Say: **What super memories you have! Find someone in another group and pat that person on the back.** Be sure everyone's been affirmed.

Hold up the Bible and say: **Our Bible story today comes from the book of 1 Kings in the Bible.** Open the *Bible Big Book: Elijah & the Big Showdown* to page 1. Say: **Our Big Book shows us pictures of the Bible story. We'll listen to the exciting story on the *CD*. Let's begin at the first page.**

Turn on the CD player and listen to pages 1 through 4, turning the pages at the sound of the chimes. At the end of page 4, turn off the CD player.

Close the *Bible Big Book.* Ask:

● **God had said he'd stop the rain. Did he? For how long?** (Yes, for three years.)

● **How did stopping the rain show God's power?** (Only God can start and stop the rain; God showed he controls the weather.)

● **Do you think King Ahab believed God was the only God? Explain.** (No, he still didn't believe it; no, he thought the fake gods were just as powerful.)

● **What showdown was going to take place?** (A showdown between Elijah and King Ahab; between the fake gods and our God.)

Say: **Elijah knew that  God is powerful, and he's the only true God. Elijah wanted the people to know that the gods they worshiped were fake. So Elijah challenged King Ahab and his men to a showdown between their phony gods and the one true God.** Ask:

● **What were they both going to do?** (Build altars; light fires and see who was more powerful.)

● **Why did God want there to be a showdown?** (So he could show he is the one true God; so people would worship the real God.)

Say: **This is a very exciting story, isn't it? Next week we'll hear more. I'm glad that we serve the only real God. Let's play a game to see if you can find what's real and what's fake.**

Do the Bible Story (up to 10 minutes)

Before class, purchase or pick a few fresh flowers that have a pleasant fragrance. Place the real flowers in one vase and silk flowers in another vase.

Set the flowers on a table and gather children around it. Say: **Let's see if you can tell real flowers from phony ones. I'll choose a couple of you to blindfold. Then you'll use your sense of smell to put the flowers to the sniff test. We'll have you smell each bouquet. When you think you know which is real, say, "Now _that's_ the real thing!"**

Choose two children to be the vase holders. Blindfold two other children and let them each smell the bouquets. Continue until everyone's had a chance to smell the flowers. Ask:

● **How did you know which flowers were real?** (By the way they smelled.)

● **Did the fake flowers look or smell like real ones?** (No, they especially didn't smell like real ones; they kind of looked real but they didn't smell real.)

Say: **Sometimes it's hard to tell when something's real or fake. Then you have to put it to the test just like we put the flowers to the sniff test. In our Bible story, Elijah wanted to put King Ahab's fake gods to the test by seeing if they could light a fire. It's important to know that 🌀 God is powerful, and he's the only true God. We don't want to be fooled—we want to worship the only true God. Let's sing a new song about the one true God.**

● **The Point**

Lead the children in singing "One True God" (track 11) with the *CD* to the tune of "Ten Little Indians." Do the accompanying motions for extra fun.

Sing 🎵

I will al-ways o-bey you, God. *(Reach hands to heaven.)*
You're the one and only true God. *(Hold up one finger.)*
I'll do what you ask me to, God. *(Nod your head.)*
You're the one true God! *(Hold up one finger.)*

Elijah always obeyed you, God. *(Reach hands to heaven.)*
He knew you're the only true God. *(Hold up one finger.)*
I will be just like him, too, God. *(Nod your head.)*
You're the one true God. *(Hold up one finger.)*

I will al-ways o-bey you, God. *(Reach hands to heaven.)*
You're the one and only true God. *(Hold up one finger.)*
I'll do what you ask me to, God. *(Nod your head.)*
You're the one true God! *(Hold up one finger.)*

✔ For a variation, point upward instead of singing the word "God" or stand up quickly on the word "God," then sit down.

God is powerful.

Say: **We want everyone to know that there's only one true God. Let's see what Pockets is up to and if she knows who's the one true God.**

Practicing the Point

True Blue (up to 5 minutes)

Before this activity, tape a real flower in Pockets' paw.

Bring out Pockets the Kangaroo and go through the following puppet script. When you finish the script, put Pockets away and out of sight.

True Blue

PUPPET SCRIPT

Pockets: *(Hopping out slowly)* Ohhhh. I hope this makes him feel better. I hope this flower helps cheer him up.

Teacher: Hello, Pockets. Who are you so worried about? Who do you want to cheer up?

Pockets: Our one blue God. I heard you talking about our blue God, and I know when you're blue you're sad. I don't want God to be sad; I want him to be happy so I have a flower for him.

Teacher: Oh, Pockets, that's really nice. But I think you misunderstood. We've been learning that  God is powerful, and he's the one <u>true</u> God—not blue God! Children, let's tell Pockets about the Bible story and about the great showdown there's going to be.

(Encourage children to tell Pockets that we serve only one God and our God is the only true God. Explain that God wants us to worship only him. Have children tell Pockets The Point.)

Teacher: Just like your flower is real, God is real, too. In fact  God is powerful, and he's the only true God. God is happy that we want to worship only him—and I think he's also happy that you wanted to give him a flower. That shows lots of love.

Pockets: Yes, real flowers are nice, but our real God is the best—and I'm glad God isn't blue. Thanks for teaching me that there's only one true God. And here's a flower for you! *(Hands flower to you.)* 'Bye everyone. See you next week!

● **The Point**

● **The Point**

God is powerful.

TODAY I LEARNED...

We believe that Christian education extends beyond the classroom into the home. Photocopy the "Today I Learned..." handout (p. 98) for this week and send it home with your children. Encourage parents to use the handout to plan meaningful family activities to reinforce this week's topic. Follow up the "Today I Learned..." activities next week by asking children what their families did.

Closing

Real Thank You's (up to 5 minutes)

Gather children in a circle. Hold the real flower from the last activity. Say: **Isn't it great to love the only true God? And we know that God loves us, too. Let's use this real flower to give God a real thank you. I'll say, "I love you, God," then I'll pass the flower to the next person.** Continue around the circle until everyone's held the flower.

Say: **Find a friend.** Pause for children to form pairs. **Decide who will go first. When I clap once, put your hand on your partner's shoulder and say, "Our God is true and God loves you."** Lead children in repeating the affirmation. Then clap again and have children affirm their partners.

Say: **Join hands with your partners and let's pray.** Pray: **Dear God, thank you for being the one true God. We know you're all-powerful and there's no one like you. We love you so much. In Jesus' name, amen.**

God is powerful.

For Extra Time

If you have a long class time or want to add additional elements to your lesson, try one of the following activities:

LIVELY LEARNING: The Real McCoy!

Choose two or three children to stand in a huddle and secretly decide who will be the Mystery Person. Then have them sit in a row while the rest of the class tries to determine who the person is by asking yes and no questions such as "Are you a girl?" or "Do you wear glasses?" When someone thinks he or she knows who the Mystery Person is, have them say the name aloud. Then ask "Will the Mystery Person please stand up?" Before choosing three new players to stand up front, talk about the fact that just as there's only one Anne or Charles, there's only one God. Then remind children that ✐ God is powerful, and he's the only true God.

● **The Point**

MAKE TO TAKE: Bumper Stickers

Before this activity, cut white contact paper into 12×3-inch strips. With a permanent marker, write "God is #1" on each paper strip.

Hand out the blank bumper stickers. Let children decorate them with colorful markers. As they work remind them that it's important to remember that ✐ God is powerful, and he's the one true God. Tell children to put their bumper stickers on wagons, bikes, or backpacks so everyone will know that they serve the one true God. Tell children to ask their parents' permission before sticking them to a car.

● **The Point**

TREAT TO EAT: Stone Tablets

Set up an assembly line and create edible "stone tablets" to help children remember that God wants us to worship only one God—him.

You'll need three groups: the Stone Cutters, Stone Spreaders, and the One-sies. The Stone Cutters will break graham crackers into squares. The Stone Spreaders will spread peanut butter on the crackers. And the One-sies will make number 1's using four M&M's on each "stone tablet." As children enjoy eating their snacks, remind them that God's first commandment says we're to have no other gods except the one true God.

> **Note:**
> Before preparing the snacks, make sure children are not allergic to the ingredients.

STORY PICTURE: Elijah Challenges King Ahab to a Great Showdown

Photocopy the story picture on page 98 for each child. Set out markers, glue, and sequins. Have children color the pictures then glue sequins on King Ahab's crown.

God is powerful.

TODAY I LEARNED . . .

The Point ✏ God is powerful, and he's the only true God.

Today your child learned that God is powerful, and he's the only true God. Children heard how Elijah challenged King Ahab to a showdown between the false gods and the one true God. Children talked about how God wants them to worship only him.

Verse to Learn

"Great is our Lord and mighty in power; his understanding has no limit" (Psalm 147:5).

Ask Me . . .

● Why was King Ahab angry with Elijah?
● How can we worship the one true God?
● How do we know our God is the one true God?

Family Fun

● Try this activity to reinforce the fact that God is the only true God. Take turns with your child looking in a mirror. Talk about how the face you see in the mirror is just a reflection—it looks like the real thing but the reflection is not really you. Tell your child that there's only one true God and we want to worship only him. Then go on a search around the house to find other things that aren't the "real thing" but just imitations, such as silk flowers, artificial flavorings, and wood veneer.

Elijah Challenges King Ahab to a Showdown (1 Kings 18:16-21)

The Power of Prayer

LESSON 7

The Point

✏ God is powerful and answers our prayers.

The Bible Basis

1 Kings 18:22-38. Elijah prayed to God and defeated the prophets of Baal in a showdown on Mount Carmel.

In a series of difficult and dangerous confrontations with wicked King Ahab, Elijah carefully followed God's leading. From making the initial announcement that there would be no rain, to taking shelter at the brook and the widow's home, then returning to face Ahab and issue a challenge, Elijah proved to be a faithful prophet. God rewarded Elijah's trust and obedience with miracle after miracle. So when he'd built an altar to God, no wonder Elijah had confidence to pray in front of hundreds of people for God to send fire to consume the water-soaked sacrifice. God answered Elijah's prayer with a fireball so astounding and terrifying that all the spectators trembled, fell to their knees, and proclaimed, "The Lord—he is God!"

Most kindergartners have yet to discover the awesome power of prayer. Many young children tend to think of prayer as something that brings them good luck. We want to teach our young children that we don't need good luck when we put our faith in God. Prayer is the key to seeking God's help, and God always answers prayer.

Getting the Point

✏ **God is powerful and answers our prayers.**

It's important to say The Point just as it's written in each activity. Repeating The Point over and over will help the children remember it and apply it to their lives.

Children will
- know that God hears and answers us when we pray,
- discover that prayer is a way of talking to God,
- teach Pockets that God answers prayers in amazing ways, and
- pray to God for his help in their lives.

✏ **The Point**

This Lesson at a Glance

Before the lesson, collect the necessary items for the activities you plan to use. Refer to the Classroom Supplies and Learning Lab Supplies columns to determine what you'll need. Remember to make photocopies of the "Today I Learned..." handout (p. 110) to send home with your children.

Section	Minutes	What Children Will Do	Classroom Supplies	Learning Lab Supplies
Welcome Time	up to 5	**Welcome!**—Receive name tags and be greeted by the teacher.	"Family Name Tags" handouts (p. 29), markers, pins or tape	
Let's Get Started Direct children to one or more of the Let's Get Started activities until everyone arrives.	up to 10	**Option 1: Build It Up**—Build a pretend altar and learn more about Elijah's altar.	Boxes or blocks	
	up to 10	**Option 2: Stone's Throw**—Play a fun target game and learn that Elijah used 12 stones to build an altar to God.	Markers, 12 small stones, masking tape	Cardboard insert from Learning Lab, pretend rock
	up to 10	**Option 3: Prayer Pals**—Decorate their own "prayer pals" to remind them to pray.	Smooth stones, glue, wiggly eyes, markers, 3x5 cards	
Pick-Up Song	up to 5	**We Will Pick Up**—Sing a song as they pick up toys and gather for Bible-Story Time.	CD player	CD: "We Will Pick Up" (track 2)
Bible-Story Time	up to 5	**Setting the Stage**—Find out that God lit a special fire and answered Elijah's prayer.	Large candle in a holder, matches, one stone, one twig, small glass of water, bag of marshmallows	
	up to 5	**Bible Song and Prayer Time**—Sing a song, bring out the Bible, and pray together.	Bible, construction paper, scissors, basket or box, CD player	CD: "God's Book" (track 3), power stamp and ink pad
	up to 10	**Hear the Bible Story**—Help tell about the exciting "showdown" from 1 Kings 18:22-38.	Bible, red construction paper, scissors, CD player	*Bible Big Book: Elijah & the Big Showdown* (pp. 5-7), CD: "Elijah & the Big Showdown" (track 12), power stamp and ink pad
	up to 10	**Do the Bible Story**—Sing an action rap about God, who's more powerful than anything!	CD player	CD: "Hands Down!" (track 13)
Practicing the Point	up to 5	**Fire Up**—Help Pockets learn that God answers prayer in amazing ways.	Pockets the Kangaroo, fireman's hat	Fish squirter
Closing	up to 5	**Partner Prayers**—Affirm their prayer partners and pray together.	Prayer pals from Option 3	
For Extra Time		For extra-time ideas and supplies, see page 109.		

God is powerful.

Welcome Time

Welcome! (up to 5 minutes)

- Bend down and make eye contact with children as they arrive.
- Greet each child individually with an enthusiastic smile.
- Thank each child for coming to class today.
- Ask children about last week's "Today I Learned..." discussion. Ask questions such as "How did you see God's power last week?" and "In what ways did you obey God?"
- Say: **Today we're going to learn that**  **God is powerful and answers our prayers.**
- Hand out the "Family" name tags children made in the first lesson and help them attach the name tags to their clothing. If some of the name tags were damaged or if some of the children weren't in class that week, have them make new name tags using the photocopiable patterns on page 29.
- Direct children to the Let's Get Started activities you've set up.

● **The Point**

Let's Get Started

Set up one or more of the following activities for children to do as they arrive. After you greet each child, invite him or her to choose an activity.

Circulate among the children to offer help as needed and direct children's conversation toward today's lesson. Ask questions such as "How do we know God hears us when we pray?" and "Does God answer our prayers?"

OPTION 1: Build It Up (up to 10 minutes)

Before class, collect an assortment of medium and large boxes or blocks.

As children arrive, invite them to build with the boxes or blocks. Suggest building things from different Bible stories, such as the walls of Jericho and Noah's ark. Then tell children that in Bible days, people worshiped God by building altars to him. Encourage children to pretend that the boxes are large, heavy stones and let them build a pretend altar to God.

As they work together, explain that people built altars to honor God and help them pray. Tell children that ● God is powerful and answers our prayers. Mention that in today's Bible story they'll learn about a time Elijah prayed and built an altar to God.

● **The Point**

OPTION 2: Stone's Throw (up to 10 minutes)

Before class, remove the cardboard insert from the Learning Lab. Use a marker to draw three concentric circles on one side of the insert. Label the innermost circle with the number 3 and set the *pretend rock* in the very center. Label the middle circle with the number 2 and the outer circle with the number 1.

Lay the cardboard target on the floor against the wall. Place a piece of masking tape 3 feet away from the game board. Set 12 small stones behind the line. Invite children to equally divide up the stones then gently toss them onto the target. Tell children that there's one rule: no one tosses until everyone is standing behind the tape. If they hit the *pretend rock* in the center circle, have children shout, "God is powerful!" After the stones are tossed, help children add up the number of points they made.

As children play, mention that in today's Bible story Elijah used 12 stones to build an altar to God. Explain that they'll hear about the amazing thing God did with that stone altar when Elijah prayed. Tell children that God is powerful and answers our prayers.

The Point

□ **OPTION 3: Prayer Pals (up to 10 minutes)**

Before class, gather a smooth, medium-sized stone for each child. Be sure the stones are clean and dry.

Set out markers, white craft glue, 3×5 cards, and wiggly eyes. Let children create "prayer pals" from the stones. Have them glue on wiggly eyes then use the markers to add other features such as noses, mouths, and hair. Help children write "Pray every day!" on 3×5 cards then glue their prayer pals to the cards.

The Point

While children make their prayer pals, explain that God is happy when we pray. Point out that prayer is like talking to God and that God is powerful and answers our prayers. Tell children that they'll hear a story about a time Elijah prayed to God and God answered his prayer in an amazing way. Tell them that their prayer pals will remind them to pray every day. Set the stones aside to dry.

> ✔ If not everyone chooses to do Option 3, have willing children make extra prayer pals to share. You'll use them in the Closing.

When everyone has arrived and you're ready to move on to the Bible-Story Time, encourage the children to finish what they're doing and get ready to clean up.

Pick-Up Song

We Will Pick Up (up to 5 minutes)

Lead children in singing "We Will Pick Up" (track 2) with the *CD* to the tune of "London Bridge." Encourage children to sing along as they help clean up the room.

If you want to include the names of all the children in your class, sing the song without the *CD* and repeat the naming section. If you choose to use the *CD*, vary the names you use each week.

Sing

We will pick up all our toys,
All our toys, all our toys.
We will pick up all our toys
And put them all away.

I see (name) picking up,
Picking up, picking up.
I see (name) picking up
And putting toys away.

(Repeat.)

Bible-Story Time

Setting the Stage (up to 5 minutes)

Tell the children you'll clap your hands to get their attention. Explain that when you clap your hands, the children are to stop what they're doing, raise their hands, and focus on you. Practice this signal a few times. Encourage children to respond quickly so you'll have time for all the fun activities you've planned.

Before this activity, set the following items on a table: a stone, a twig, a clear glass of water, a bag of marshmallows, a candle in a holder, and matches.

Gather the children around the table. Light the candle. Hold up the twig. Ask:

● **Can fire burn a twig? Why?** (Yes, because it's wood.)

● **What other things on this table could fire burn?** (The marshmallows; the other matches; the candle; the table.)

● **Which things won't burn?** (Water; the stone.)

Say: **We've been learning the past few weeks about God's power. We know that God is more powerful than anyone or anything. And we also know that God is powerful enough to control everything.** Ask:

● **Can God control fire, too? Why or why not?** (Yes, God's more powerful than anything, including fire; yes, God controls fire; yes, God can make fire.)

Say: **We aren't powerful enough to make fire melt stones or make water burn up—but God is! We're going to hear an exciting Bible story today about how Elijah prayed to God to light a fire.** Ask:

● **When do you pray?** (At supper time; at bedtime; any time I need help.)

● **Who can tell about a time God answered your prayers?** Allow children time to tell their experiences.

Say: **It's wonderful to know that when we pray, God always hears our prayers and answers them, too. Sometimes it takes a while, but God always answers our prayers. When Elijah prayed, God answered him in a miraculous way. God can make miracles happen when we pray.** ◖ **God is powerful and answers our prayers.**

Before we hear our story, let's repeat The Point as I blow out the candle. Then we'll pretend we just toasted some delicious marshmallows over a fire to eat! Lead children in saying The Point as you blow out the candle. Then give each child a marshmallow to eat. Set the candle and matches out of sight of the children.

✐ **The Point**

Bible Song and Prayer Time (up to 5 minutes)

Before class, make surprise cards for this activity by cutting construction paper into 2×6-inch slips. Prepare a surprise card for each child, plus a few extras for visitors. Fold the cards in half, then stamp the *power stamp* inside one of the surprise cards. Mark 1 Kings 18:22-38 in the Bible you'll be using.

Have children sit in a circle. Say: **Now it's time to choose a Bible person to bring me the Bible marked with today's Bible story. As we sing our Bible song, I'll pass out the surprise cards. Don't look inside your card until the song is over.**

Lead children in singing "God's Book" (track 3) with the *CD* to the tune of "Old MacDonald Had a Farm." As you sing, pass out the folded surprise cards. If you want to include the names of all the children in your class, sing the song without the *CD* and repeat the naming section. If you choose to use the *CD*, vary the names you use each week.

Sing ♪♫♪♫♪

Now it's time to read God's Book
And hear a Bible story.
It's fun to be here with my
    friends
And hear a Bible story.

(Name)**'s here.**
(Name)**'s here.**
Here is (name).
Here is (name).
Now it's time to read God's Book
And hear a Bible story.

Now it's time to read God's Book
And hear a Bible story.
It's fun to be here with my
    friends
And hear a Bible story.

(Name)**'s here.**
(Name)**'s here.**
Here is (name).
Here is (name).
Now it's time to read God's Book
And hear a Bible story.

After the song, say: **You may look inside your surprise cards. The person who has power stamped inside his or her card will be our Bible person for today.**

Identify the Bible person, then have the rest of the children clap for him or her. Ask the Bible person to bring you the Bible. Help the Bible person open the Bible to the marked place and show children where your story comes from. Then have the Bible person sit down.

● **The Point**

Say: (Name) **was our special Bible person today. Each week, we'll have only one special Bible person, but each one of you is a special part of our class! Today we're all learning that** ● **God is powerful and answers our prayers.**

Let's say a special prayer now and ask God to help us remember to pray. I'll pass around this basket. When the basket comes to you, put your surprise card in it and say, "God, please remind me to pray."

Pass around the basket or box. When you've collected everyone's surprise card, set the basket aside and pick up the Bible. Lead children in this prayer:

● **The Point**

God, thank you for the Bible and all the stories in it. Teach us today that ● **you are powerful and answer our prayers. Amen.**

       God is powerful.

Hear the Bible Story (up to 10 minutes)

Before this activity, cut a flame from red construction paper for each child.

Open the Bible to 1 Kings 18:22-38. Say: **Our Bible story comes from the book of 1 Kings in the Bible. We've been hearing the exciting story of Elijah, God's prophet. Let's see if you remember what's happened so far. Get with a friend.** Pause while children form pairs or trios. Open the *Bible Big Book: Elijah & the Big Showdown* to page 1. **I'll ask a story question about the picture you see. Then I'll choose a pair of friends to answer the question and point to the part of the picture that tells about the answer.** Ask the following questions:

Page 1:
- **Who was God's special prophet?** (Elijah.)
- **Why was God angry at wicked King Ahab?** (Ahab didn't love God; he worshiped idols.)
- **What did Elijah tell King Ahab?** (That God would stop the rain.)

Pages 2-3:
- **Where did God hide Elijah?** (By a riverbank; near a river.)
- **How did the ravens know to feed Elijah every day?** (God sent them.)
- **How did God work through Elijah to help the widow?** (He gave her flour and oil that would never run out; he raised her son from the dead.)
- **How did the widow know that God answers prayer?** (Because she was hungry and God kept her flour and oil from running out.)

Page 4:
- **What challenge did Elijah make King Ahab?** (To see if his god could light a fire.)
- **Whose God is powerful and always answers prayer?** (Our God.)

Close the Big Book. Say: **Great job everybody! You always listen well to the Bible stories! You can each stamp your hand with the *power stamp*.** Pause while children stamp their hands.

Now we'll hear the next part of the story. You can help tell the story with these paper flames. Hand out the flames. **When you hear the word "fire" on the *CD*, wave your flames.** Open the *Bible Big Book* to page 5. Turn on the CD player (track 12) and listen to the story segment, turning the page at the sound of the chimes. Turn off the CD player after page 7.

Close the Big Book. Say: **That was some fire, wasn't it? It was a fire that only God could send!** Ask:
- **What happened when King Ahab's men prayed to their fake gods?** (Nothing; the fire didn't come.)
- **How do you think King Ahab felt when his fake god didn't answer?** (Angry; madder than ever at Elijah; worried.)
- **Why did Elijah pour so much water on the altar? Wasn't he afraid it wouldn't burn?** (He wanted to show the people that God is powerful and can light any fire; Elijah wasn't afraid because he knew God is powerful.)

Say: **Elijah knew that God's power can do anything—even light sopping wet wood. God didn't want King Ahab to have any doubts that he's the one true God! And Elijah wasn't worried about the fire starting because he knew that God answers prayer.** Ask:
- **What did Elijah pray that God would do?** (Light the fire on the altar; show the people that God is the real God.)

God is powerful.

● **How did God answer Elijah?** (He sent down a huge fire; he burned up everything.)

Say: **Elijah prayed and God heard him and answered right away. Isn't it wonderful that**  **God is powerful and answers our prayers? God answered Elijah's prayers to light the altar fire. And we know that God hears and answers our prayers, too. That's because we serve a God who's more powerful than anything and will always win any challenge hands down! Let's sing a new rap song about our mighty God.**

● The Point

Do the Bible Story (up to 10 minutes)

Have children practice slapping their own knees or "patty-caking" with a friend to the line, "God will win (slap, slap)—hands down!" Then play the song "Hands Down!" (track 13) on the *CD*. Lead children in bopping around the room on the verses and singing the chorus words together.

✔ Go over the words to the chorus without the CD. Be sure children know how to slap their legs on the X's in the chorus. When the children seem familiar with the words, have them sing the entire song with the CD.

Sing

Elijah was a man of God.
When God said, "Go," Elijah'd nod.
God sent Elijah to an evil king
To show him God's more powerful than anything!

**Let us shout an' let us sing:
GOD'S MORE POWERFUL THAN ANYTHING!
There's no problem when God's around
'Cuz God will win XX—HANDS DOWN!**

"King A-hab, you're a wicked king!
You worship gods that don't mean a thing!
There's gonna be a big showdown,
But God will win XX—HANDS DOWN!

**Let us shout an' let us sing:
GOD'S MORE POWERFUL THAN ANYTHING!
There's no problem when God's around
'Cuz God will win XX—HANDS DOWN!**

So they built an altar of stone and mud,

But Ahab's god was just a <u>dud!</u>
There wasn't a <u>spark</u> of flame around!
Now God would win XX—HANDS DOWN!

**Let us shout an' let us sing:
GOD'S MORE POWERFUL THAN ANYTHING!
There's no problem when God's around
'Cuz God will win XX—HANDS DOWN!**

Then God sent a fiery flash of flame,
And the people shouted, "GOD'S HIS NAME!"
They bowed their faces to the ground!
And God had won XX—HANDS DOWN!

**Let us shout an' let us sing:
GOD'S MORE POWERFUL THAN ANYTHING!
There's no problem when God's around
'Cuz God will win XX—HANDS DOWN!**

God is powerful.

When you're finished singing, turn off the CD player. Say: **That's a fun song to remind us that 🖊 God is powerful and answers our prayers. It'll help us remember that "God will win** (slap, slap) **hands down!" Let's share that great news with Pockets, shall we?**

🖊 **The Point**

Practicing the Point

Fire Up (up to 5 minutes)

Before class, put a fireman's hat on Pockets' head or make a small red hat using red construction paper. Fill the *fish squirter* from the Learning Lab with water by squeezing it tightly then immersing it in water. Keep it submerged as you release your hold on the squirter.

Bring out Pockets the Kangaroo holding the *fish squirter*. Go through the following puppet script. When you finish the script, put Pockets away and out of sight.

Fire Up

PUPPET SCRIPT

Pockets: *(Squirting the fish squirter above the children's heads)* Where's the fire? I'll put it out! I have lots of water! I can do the job!

Teacher: Pockets, Pockets! What's going on?

Pockets: *(Hopping and squirting water)* Pockets to the rescue! I have water you know! *(Squirts you on the cheek.)*

Teacher: *(Wiping your cheek)* Yes, Pockets. We can feel your water, can't we, children? But Pockets, there's no fire here. I think you're mistaken.

Pockets: But I heard you talking about a big fire that's melting stones 'n' wood 'n' everything! How did it start? Where is it?

Teacher: Oh Pockets, the fire's not in our classroom. It happened a long time ago in Bible days. Children, let's tell Pockets about the Bible story and how God answered Elijah's prayer in an amazing way.

(Encourage children to tell about how King Ahab's fake gods didn't light the fire, but when Elijah prayed to the true God, God sent a mighty fire to show his power. Have children point out that Elijah prayed to God and God answered his prayers. Have them tell Pockets The Point.)

Pockets: Wow, that must've been sooome fire! God answered Elijah's prayer in a neat-o way. But who called the fire department to put out that big fire?

Teacher: *(Laughing)* Nobody called the fire department, Pockets! God's fire burned up the altar and stones and

(Continued)

The Point

water and meat. There was nothing left to burn. God answered Elijah's prayer when he sent the fire. And we know, just like Elijah knew, that 🖊 God is powerful and answers our prayers.

Pockets: I'm glad that we serve a powerful God. But maybe next time he puts out a fire he'll let <u>me</u> help! (Squirts water once more.) 'Bye everybody!

(Return the fish squirter to the Learning Lab.)

TODAY I LEARNED...

We believe that Christian education extends beyond the classroom into the home. Photocopy the "Today I Learned..." handout (p. 110) for this week and send it home with your children. Encourage parents to use the handout to plan meaningful family activities to reinforce this week's topic. Follow up the "Today I Learned..." activities next week by asking children what their families did.

Closing

Partner Prayers (up to 5 minutes)

The Point

Hand out the "prayer pals" children made in Option 3 and have children get with a friend. Say: **We've been learning today that 🖊 God is powerful and answers our prayers. God hears every prayer we pray. Sometimes we may not understand God's answers, but we can be sure of one thing—God always answers our prayers in the way that's best for us.**

Decide which of you will go first. Then I'll clap my hands and that person can tell one time he or she can pray to God today. When I clap my hands again, the other partner will have a turn.

After both partners have shared, say: **Now give your partner a pat on the shoulder and say, "God hears your prayers."** Pause for children to respond. **Join hands with your partner and let's pray right now.** Pray: **Dear God, we're thankful that you always answer prayer. Please help us each day of our lives like you helped Elijah when he prayed. We love you. In Jesus' name, amen.**

The Point

Take home your prayer pals to remind you to pray and to remind you that 🖊 God is powerful and answers our prayers.

For Extra Time

If you have a long class time or want to add additional elements to your lesson, try one of the following activities:

LIVELY LEARNING: **Story Scramble**

Make two large banners by taping three sheets of paper together for each banner. Tape the banners to the wall. Form two lines and hand the first person in each line a crayon. Tell children that they'll draw the story of Elijah and the big showdown. When you clap your hands, the person with the crayon hops to the banner and draws one part of the story. When you clap again, he or she hops back and the next person in line goes. Continue until each person has added a portion of the story. Then let the groups tell about their pictures. Remind children that in the story Elijah prayed for God's help, and God answered by lighting the fire at the altar. Have children say,  "God is powerful and answers our prayers."

MAKE TO TAKE: **Put Out the Fire**

Cover a table with newspapers. Fill a spray bottle or the *fish squirter* from the Learning Lab with water. Hand each child a sheet of paper. Sprinkle a little red and yellow powdered tempera paint on each paper. Let children take turns spraying their pictures and letting the paint run and mix to create different colors. Point out how the colors remind us of fire. Have children tell how God started the altar fire and remind them that even water didn't stop the fire from burning. Mention that ✎ God is powerful and answers our prayers, just like he answered Elijah's prayer by lighting the fire.

Set the pictures aside to dry.

TREAT TO EAT: **Dough Delights**

Before this activity, make edible modeling dough from the following recipe. Mix 3 cups of powdered sugar with ¾ cup peanut butter. Knead the dough to make it pliable, then store the dough in a sealed plastic bag.

Hand each child a piece of wax paper and a golf ball size lump of edible dough. Encourage children to make Bible story figures such as Elijah, the raven, flames, or stones. Then have children make prayer hands from their dough. Talk about the fact that ✎ God is powerful and answers our prayers. As children eat their dough, invite them to tell about times God answered their prayers.

STORY PICTURE: **God Answers Elijah's Prayers**

Photocopy the "Today I Learned . . ." handout from page 110 for each child. Set out glue sticks and red, orange, and yellow construction paper scraps. Have children tear flames from the colored paper to glue to their pictures. Remind children that Elijah prayed for God to light the altar fire and that ✎ God is powerful and answers our prayers.

● **The Point** ✎

● **The Point** ✎

Note:
Before preparing the snacks, make sure children are not allergic to the ingredients.

● **The Point** ✎

● **The Point** ✎

TODAY I LEARNED...

The Point ✏ God is powerful and answers our prayers.

Today your child learned that God is powerful and answers our prayers. Children learned that God answered Elijah's prayers in amazing ways. They also talked about praying every day.

Verse to Learn

"Great is our Lord and mighty in power; his understanding has no limit" (Psalm 147:5).

Ask Me...

● How did God answer Elijah's prayer?
● When is a time God answered your prayers?
● When can our family pray together?

Family Fun

● Sing "One True God" with your child to the tune of "Ten Little Indians." Then talk about how God wants us to obey and pray just as Elijah did. Share times God answered your prayers.

I will al-ways o-bey you, God. *(Reach hands to heaven.)*

You're the one and only true God. *(Hold up one finger.)*

I'll do what you ask me to, God. *(Nod your head.)*

You're the one true God! *(Hold up one finger.)*

God Answers Elijah's Prayer (1 Kings 18:22-38)

Permission to photocopy this handout from Group's Hands-On Bible Curriculum™ for Pre-K & K granted for local church use. Copyright © Group Publishing, Inc. P.O. Box 481, Loveland, CO 80539

Praise Him! Praise Him!

The Bible Basis

1 Kings 18:39. "When all the people saw this, they fell prostrate and cried, 'The Lord—he is God! The Lord—he is God!'"

When God's flash of holy fire consumed the entire altar and sacrifice Elijah had prepared, the people of Israel who had been unfaithful and disobedient to God fell to the ground. And in this humble, prostrate position, they praised God with the words: "The Lord—he is God!" In that one simple sentence, the people worshiped the name of God and acknowledged that he alone is mighty and worthy to be praised.

How often do we remind 5- and 6-year-olds to say "thank you"? Whether it's for a cookie at the bakery or help on a school project, we encourage young children to acknowledge other people's kindness and help. It's important for kindergartners to realize the joy in thanking and praising God for all he does, too. Use this lesson to teach children that there are many wonderful ways to praise God and express our love.

Getting the Point

✎ **God is powerful, and we can praise him.**

It's important to say The Point just as it's written in each activity. Repeating The Point over and over will help the children remember it and apply it to their lives.

Children will
- understand what it means to praise God,
- discover ways to praise God,
- teach Pockets that praising God is very important, and
- express their praises to God.

✎ **The Point**

This Lesson at a Glance

Before the lesson, collect the necessary items for the activities you plan to use. Refer to the Classroom Supplies and Learning Lab Supplies columns to determine what you'll need. Remember to make photocopies of the "Today I Learned…" handout (p. 122) to send home with your children.

Section	Minutes	What Children Will Do	Classroom Supplies	Learning Lab Supplies
Welcome Time	up to 5	**Welcome!**—Receive name tags and be greeted by the teacher.	"Family Name Tags" handouts (p. 29), markers, pins or tape	
Let's Get Started Direct children to one or more of the Let's Get Started activities until everyone arrives.	up to 10	**Option 1: Praise Pals**—Make life-size paper dolls and pretend to walk with them.	Roll of white shelf paper, scissors, pencils, markers, rubber bands	
	up to 10	**Option 2: Rock 'n' Roll**—Build with pretend rocks and bowl over their creations.	Building blocks, masking tape, playground ball	Pretend rock
	up to 10	**Option 3: Praise Shakers**—Create rhythm instruments to praise God.	Paper cups, duct tape, markers, curling ribbon, dry beans, scissors	Power stamp and ink pad
Pick-Up Song	up to 5	**We Will Pick Up**—Sing a song as they pick up toys and gather for Bible-Story Time.	CD player	CD: "We Will Pick Up" (track 2)
Bible-Story Time	up to 5	**Setting the Stage**—See how King Ahab's people ran then praised the one true God.	Pepper shaker, cereal bowl, pitcher of water, large bowl, liquid dish soap	
	up to 5	**Bible Song and Prayer Time**—Sing a song, bring out the Bible, and pray together.	Bible, construction paper, scissors, basket or box, CD player	CD: "God's Book" (track 3), power stamp and ink pad
	up to 10	**Hear the Bible Story**—Use the cape to help tell the Bible story from 1 Kings 18:39.	Bible	Bible Big Book: Elijah & the Big Showdown (p. 8), cape
	up to 10	**Do the Bible Story**—Sing an action praise song with their praise pals.	CD player, praise pals from Option 1	CD: "Hands Down!" (track 13)
Practicing the Point	up to 5	**Peppery Pockets**—Teach Pockets there are different ways to praise God.	Pockets the Kangaroo, pepper shaker	
Closing	up to 5	**Joyful Praise**—Sing a joyous song and pray.	CD player, shakers from Option 3	CD: "Shout With Joy" (track 9)
For Extra Time		For extra-time ideas and supplies, see page 121.		

God is powerful.

Welcome Time

Welcome! (up to 5 minutes)

- Bend down and make eye contact with children as they arrive.
- Greet each child individually with an enthusiastic smile.
- Thank each child for coming to class today.
- Ask children about last week's "Today I Learned..." discussion. Ask questions such as "Who's more powerful than anyone or anything?"
- Say: **Today we're going to learn that  God is powerful, and we can praise him.**
- Hand out the "Family" name tags children made in Lesson 1 and help them attach the name tags to their clothing. If some of the name tags were damaged or if some of the children weren't in class that week, have them make new name tags using the photocopiable patterns on page 29.
- Direct children to the Let's Get Started activities you've set up.

● The Point

Let's Get Started

Set up one or more of the following activities for children to do as they arrive. After you greet each child, invite him or her to choose an activity.

Circulate among the children to offer help as needed and direct children's conversation toward today's lesson. Ask questions such as "How can we praise God?" and "How can we thank God for all he does?"

OPTION 1: Praise Pals (up to 10 minutes)

Set out a roll of white shelf paper, pencils, markers, scissors, and rubber bands. As children arrive invite them to lie on the paper. Then trace around each child to make a life-size paper "praise pal." Help children cut out the paper pals, then allow children to color their pals with markers. As they work, ask questions such as "When someone helps you what do you say?" and "When's a time you thanked someone for doing something nice for you?" Mention that in today's Bible story, people found out that ● God is powerful, and we can praise him. Point out that if everyone in class makes a praise pal there will be quite a crowd! Explain to children that their crowd of special pals will help them to praise God later.

When the pals are colored, help children bend the paper feet forward at the ankles. Slip rubber bands over the paper foot and the child's foot, securing them together. Let children walk around the room "hand in hand" with their pals. Then set the praise pals by the wall to rest.

● The Point

✔ If possible, have each child make a praise pal to use in the "Setting the Stage" activity. Life-size paper dolls are highly motivating but time consuming. You may wish to use only two Options for this class time.

God is powerful.

Lesson 8 ● 113

Option 2: Rock 'n' Roll (up to 10 minutes)

Set out 12 building blocks near a wall. Lay a strip of masking tape about 5 feet from the wall as a starting line. Set a playground ball behind the starting line. Encourage children to pretend the blocks are rocks and build something to knock over. Have children set the *pretend rock* on the very top of their building. Then have them take turns rolling the ball from behind the starting line to bowl over the "rocks." As they play, remind children that Elijah built an altar to God, then prayed for God to light the altar fire. When God answered Elijah's prayer, the altar burned down. Mention that in today's Bible story the people were amazed at God's power and praised him. The people knew that ● God is powerful, and we can praise him.

● **The Point**

Option 3: Praise Shakers (up to 10 minutes)

Set out paper cups, dry beans, markers, duct tape, scissors, curling ribbon, and the *power stamp and ink pad*. Hand each child two paper cups. Demonstrate how to place a few dry beans in one cup, then tape the cups rim to rim using a piece of duct tape. Encourage children to help each other tape their cups. Have them use markers and the *power stamp* to decorate their shakers. Then help children cut and curl lengths of curling ribbon. Tape the ribbon curls to the center of the shaker.

● **The Point**

While children work, make comments such as "I'm glad that ● God is powerful, and we can praise him" and "Music is a good way to praise God." Explain that the shakers will be used to praise God in a later activity. Be sure children's names are on the shakers.

When everyone has arrived and you're ready to move on to the Bible-Story Time, encourage the children to finish what they're doing and get ready to clean up.

Pick-Up Song

We Will Pick Up (up to 5 minutes)

Lead children in singing "We Will Pick Up" (track 2) with the *CD* to the tune of "London Bridge." Encourage children to sing along as they help clean up the room.

If you want to include the names of all the children in your class, sing the song without the *CD* and repeat the naming section. If you choose to use the *CD*, vary the names you use each week.

Sing

We will pick up all our toys,	I see (name) picking up,
All our toys, all our toys.	Picking up, picking up.
We will pick up all our toys	I see (name) picking up
And put them all away.	And putting toys away.

(Repeat.)

God is powerful.

Bible-Story Time

Setting the Stage (up to 5 minutes)

Tell the children you'll clap your hands to get their attention. Explain that when you clap your hands, the children are to stop what they're doing, raise their hands, and focus on you. Practice this signal a few times. Encourage children to respond quickly so you'll have time for all the fun activities you've planned.

Before this activity, set out a full pitcher of water, a cereal bowl, a pepper shaker, liquid dish soap, and an empty bucket or large bowl.

Say: **In the Bible story last week, Elijah built an altar to God from 12 stones.** Set the empty cereal bowl down. **Remember how he poured 12 jars of water over the altar?** Half fill the bowl with water. Sprinkle pepper gently in the center of the bowl so it floats on top of the water. Say: **King Ahab and all the people waited for Elijah's God to light the altar. Elijah prayed and what happened?** Pause for children to tell their ideas.

God's fire burned the altar! Place one drop of liquid dish soap in the center of the pepper. **The people backed away from the great fire. They finally knew who was the true God! Did you see them back away in awe and amazement? Think of what they felt like when their fake gods didn't light the fire but God burned everything in a flash! Would you like to make the people scatter, too?**

Empty the old water into the bucket or large bowl. Pour a bit more water from the pitcher into the bowl. Let children sprinkle their own pepper "people" in the center then drip a drop of soap in. Continue until everyone's had a turn. Then ask:

● **Why did God show his great power to the people?** (He wanted them to know he was the real God; he wanted them to worship only him.)

Say: **God didn't want the people to worship fake gods. God wanted them to worship only him. So God showed his mighty power.** Ask:

● **Do you think the people praised God? Why or why not?** (Yes, they knew who the true God is; no, they were too scared.)

Say: **In the Bible story today, we'll find out what those amazed people did after God's fabulous fire. We know who the true God is and that** ⬦ **God is powerful, and we can praise him. We'll see if King Ahab's people learned the same thing.**

Bible Song and Prayer Time (up to 5 minutes)

Before class, make surprise cards for this activity by cutting construction paper into 2×6-inch slips. Prepare a surprise card for each child, plus a few extras for visitors. Fold the cards in half, then stamp the *power stamp* inside one of the surprise cards. Mark 1 Kings 18:39 in the Bible you'll be using.

Have children sit in a circle. Say: **Now it's time to choose a Bible person to bring me the Bible marked with today's Bible story. As we sing our Bible song, I'll pass out the surprise cards. Don't look inside your card until the song is over.**

Lead children in singing "God's Book" (track 3) with the *CD* to the tune of "Old MacDonald Had a Farm." As you sing, pass out the folded surprise cards.

⬦ **The Point**

If you want to include the names of all the children in your class, sing the song without the *CD* and repeat the naming section. If you choose to use the *CD,* vary the names you use each week.

Sing

Now it's time to read God's Book	Now it's time to read God's Book
And hear a Bible story.	And hear a Bible story.
It's fun to be here with my	It's fun to be here with my
friends	friends
And hear a Bible story.	And hear a Bible story.
(Name)**'s here.**	(Name)**'s here.**
(Name)**'s here.**	(Name)**'s here.**
Here is (name).	**Here is** (name).
Here is (name).	**Here is** (name).
Now it's time to read God's Book	Now it's time to read God's Book
And hear a Bible story.	And hear a Bible story.

After the song, say: **You may look inside your surprise cards. The person who has power stamped inside his or her card will be our Bible person for today.**

Identify the Bible person, then have the rest of the children clap for him or her. Ask the Bible person to bring you the Bible. Help the Bible person open the Bible to the marked place and show children where your story comes from. Then have the Bible person sit down.

Say: (Name) **was our special Bible person today. Each week, we'll have only one special Bible person, but each one of you is a special part of our class! Today we're all learning that** ⬤ **God is powerful, and we can praise him.**

Let's say a special prayer now and ask God to help us remember to pray. I'll pass around this basket. When the basket comes to you, put your surprise card in it and say, "I want to praise you, God."

⬤ **The Point**

Pass around the basket or box. When you've collected everyone's surprise card, set the basket aside and pick up the Bible. Lead children in this prayer: **God, thank you for the Bible and all the stories in it. Teach us today that** ⬤ **you are powerful, and we can praise you. Amen.**

⬤ **The Point**

Hear the Bible Story (up to 10 minutes)

Bring out the *Bible Big Book: Elijah & the Big Showdown.* Put on the *cape* from the Learning Lab. Say: **We'll pretend this is Elijah's cape or coat and use it to help tell the Bible story today. We'll pass the** *cape* **around the circle. When I say "stop," the person with the** *cape* **may put it on, then jump up and say, "God is powerful!" Then we'll continue passing the** *cape.* Hold up the Bible. **Our Bible story comes from 1 Kings 18:39 in the Bible.** Hold up the Big Book. **Our Big Book shows us pictures of what happened in the story.** Open the Big Book to page 8. Read the following story portion as you pass the *cape* around the circle.

When they saw the fiery explosion, the terrified people fell to the ground in fear and wonder. Stop. Pause for child with the *cape* to stand, put on the *cape,* and repeat The Point. Then continue reading and passing the *cape.*

...ied. Stop.** Pause.

...**people learned that our**

...**fire to burn up the al-**
...**d serve today. Stop.**
...**nds for our pow**...**op.** Pause, then lead
...g. **Hooray! Our God is the**...**God—hooray!**
...e *Big Book* and set the *cape* aside...

...**d the people do when they saw the**...**fire?** (They fell to
...; they worshiped God; they praised God.)

...**remembers what words the people cried**...**t?** ("The Lord is

...**Why are those words so special?** (They showed th... the people knew
...the real God is; they called God by his name.)

...ay: **It didn't take long for those people to know who the real God is,**
...**it? They knew right away, and they began to praise God right then**
...**d there. We know who the real God is, too. And we know that**
...**God is powerful, and we can praise him.** Ask:

The Point

● **What does it mean to praise God?** (To worship God; to tell God we love
him; to tell people about the great things God does.)

● **Why do we want to praise God?** (To tell God we love him; because he's
God; so others will know about God's power.)

● **What are some ways we can praise God?** (By praying; by telling others about how great God is; by singing.)

Say: **There are lots of ways to praise God and tell him we love him and**
know he is God. One good way is to sing. Let's sing the song we learned
last week to remind us how God wins any challenge hands down. Let's
use our praise pals to help us sing and praise God.

Return the *cape* and *Bible Big Book* to the Learning Lab.

Do the Bible Story (up to 10 minutes)

Hand out the praise pals children made in Option 1. Have them slip the rubber bands over their shoes so the dolls can move with them. Tell them to hold
"hands" with their praise pals and practice gently slapping their knees to the
line "God will win (slap, slap)—hands down!" Tell children to be careful not to
tear their paper dolls.

Play the song "Hands Down!" (track 13) on the *CD*. Lead children in bopping around the room with their praise pals on the verses, then singing the
chorus together.

Elijah was a man of God.
When God said, "Go," Elijah'd nod.
God sent Elijah to an evil king
To show him God's more powerful
   than anything!

Let us shout an' let us sing:
GOD'S MORE POWERFUL THAN
   ANYTHING!
There's no problem when
   God's around

'Cuz God will win XX—HANDS
   DOWN!

"King A-hab, you're a wicked
   king!
You worship gods that don't
   mean a thing!
There's gonna be a big showdown,
But God will win XX—HANDS
   DOWN!

Let us shout an' let us sing:
GOD'S MORE POWERFUL THAN
   ANYTHING!
There's no problem when
God's around
'Cuz God will win XX—HANDS
   DOWN!

So they built an altar of stone
   and mud,
But Ahab's god was just a <u>dud</u>!
There wasn't a <u>spark</u> of flame
   around!
Now God would win XX—HANDS
DOWN!

Let us shout an' let us sing:
GOD'S MORE POWERFUL THAN
   ANYTHING!
There's no problem when
   God's around

'Cuz God will win XX—HANDS
   DOWN!
Then God sent a fiery flash of
   flame,
And the people shouted, "GOD'S
   HIS NAME!"
They bowed their faces to the
   ground!
And God had won XX—HANDS
   DOWN!

Let us shout an' let us sing:
GOD'S MORE POWERFUL THAN
   ANYTHING!
There's no problem when
   God's around
'Cuz God will win XX—HANDS
   DOWN!

🖉 **The Point**

Say: **It's fun to praise God. And the best part about praising God is that we can praise him any time! It's important to know that** 🖉 **God is powerful and we can praise him whenever we want.** Pause and make a muffled sneezing sound. **Oh, that was a funny sound. Do you think that was Pockets? Let's see what she's up to.**

Practicing the Point

Peppery Pockets (up to 5 minutes)

Place the pepper shaker in Pockets' pouch. Then bring out Pockets the Kangaroo and go through the following puppet script. When you finish the script, put Pockets away and out of sight.

Peppery Pockets

PUPPET SCRIPT

Pockets: *(Hopping up each time she sneezes)* AahhCHOOO! Aaahchoo!

Teacher: *Pockets? That's a different kind of praising. We can see you hop up and down—you must be very happy.*

Pockets: *Aaahchhoo! Aahchoooey!*

(Continued)

God is powerful.

Teacher: Yes, we've been talking about praising and how happy it makes us. We've even been learning different ways to praise God, but you have a new way, doesn't she, children?

Pockets: I...I...aahchhhchhhCHOOOOOO!

Teacher: My goodness! Are you <u>sneezing,</u> Pockets? What's this in here?(Reaches in her pouch and pulls out the pepper.) Oh! The pepper!

Pockets: AhhCHHOO! Thank you. I guess that pepper was tickling my nose. I wanted to try making the people run then praise God—but the only thing that got runny was my nose! (Giggling)

Teacher: Yes, we did use pepper to show what the people in our Bible story did. But they did something much more important, too. Children, can you tell Pockets what the people did when they fell to the ground?

   (Encourage children to tell Pockets how the people praised God and called him by name. Have children point out that the people finally knew who was the real God and they wanted to praise him. Lead children in saying The Point.)

Teacher: We want to praise God, too, Pockets. We sang a neat song to praise God, and we're going to learn more ways to praise him.

Pockets: I'm glad to know about praising God. I guess sneezing to praise God might be fine if you have a cold. But singing is a lot prettier. Say, do you think I can borrow this pepper? I'd still like to try that little trick you guys did. (Stuffs the pepper in her pouch and hops off sneezing.) Ahchhooo—aahhh-chooooey!

Teacher: (Shaking your head) 'Bye, Pockets.

TODAY I LEARNED . . .

   We believe that Christian education extends beyond the classroom into the home. Photocopy the "Today I Learned . . ." handout (p. 122) for this week and send it home with your children. Encourage parents to use the handout to plan meaningful family activities to reinforce this week's topic. Follow up the "Today I Learned . . ." activities next week by asking children what their families did.

God is powerful.

Closing

Joyful Praise (up to 5 minutes)

● **The Point**

Gather children in a circle. Say: **We've been learning today that** ◐ **God is powerful, and we can praise him. Praising God makes us so joyful! That's how it is with praising God. Praising him makes us want to clap and march around and shout with joy. Let's sing an exciting praise song that's filled with joy!** Hand out the praise shakers children made in Option 3. If you chose not to do this Option, clap your hands instead.

Lead children in singing "Shout With Joy" (track 9) with the *CD* to the tune of "Old MacDonald Had a Farm." Shake your praise shakers or clap in time to the music.

Sing

Clap your hands now, ev'ryone.
Shout to God with joy . . . JOY!
The Lord our God is powerful.
Shout to God with joy . . . JOY!

Clap your hands.
March around.
Jump up high.
Now bend down.
Clap your hands now, ev'ryone.
Shout to God with joy . . . JOY!

(Repeat.)

Say: **Singing is a good way to praise God and so is praying. Let's praise God with a prayer.** Pray: **Dear God, we know you alone are the one true God. We thank you for your power and your love. Help us remember to praise you every day. In Jesus' name, amen.**

God is powerful.

For Extra Time

If you have a long class time or want to add additional elements to your lesson, try one of the following activities:

LIVELY LEARNING: Bible Big Book Listening Center

Set out the CD player with the *CD* cued to the *Bible Big Book* story of "Elijah & the Big Showdown." The entire story is track 14 on the *CD*. Let two children hold the *Bible Big Book* and turn the pages at the sound of the chimes. Keep track of which children have been page turners so each child will have a turn sometime during the year.

MAKE TO TAKE: Praise Kazoos

Let the children decorate an empty bathroom tissue paper tube or 3-inch section of paper-toweling tube with markers. Then fasten a 4-inch square of wax paper on one end of the tube with a rubber band. Invite the children to hum into the open ends of their "praise kazoos" to make music. Have a marching praise band and use the shakers made in Option 3 along with the kazoos. Remind children that making music is a good way to praise God and that ✎ God is powerful, and we can praise him.

● The Point

TREAT TO EAT: Party Praise Pudding

Hand each child a paper cup and a craft stick or plastic spoon. Pour 3 tablespoons of instant vanilla pudding into each paper cup. Fill the cup almost full with milk and let the children stir their treats for one minute. Set the cups down as you talk about ways to praise God and allow the pudding to thicken a bit. Then let children add colorful sprinkles to the top of their pudding. As they enjoy eating their party snacks, remind children that ✎ God is powerful, and we can praise him. Point out that when we praise God, it gives us a joyous party feeling inside.

● The Point

STORY PICTURE: The People Praise God

Photocopy the "Today I Learned . . ." handout from page 122 for each child. Set out crayons, glue, and alphabet cereal or noodles. Have children color their pictures then glue letters to spell the word "God" in the conversation bubbles above the people's heads. Read the people's words aloud and remind children that calling God's name is a way to praise him. Have children say The Point with you: ✎ "God is powerful, and we can praise him."

● The Point

God is powerful.

TODAY I LEARNED . . .

The Point 🖉 God is powerful, and we can praise him.

Today your child learned that God is powerful, and we can praise him. Children learned that Elijah helped the people know who the one true God is. They discovered different ways to praise and thank God.

Verse to Learn

"Great is our Lord and mighty in power; his understanding has no limit" (Psalm 147:5).

Ask Me . . .

● What did the people in the Bible story do when they saw God's fire burn the altar?

● What's one way you can praise God this week?

● How can our family praise God every day?

Family Fun

● Let your child make colorful praise chimes to hang. Cut streamers of crepe paper or ribbon in varying lengths from 10 to 14 inches. Tape or staple them together at the top. Help your child use twist-tie wires to fasten jingle bells to the ends of the streamers. Then hang your praise chimes in the doorway to your kitchen or living room. Each time you walk by, jangle the chimes to remind you that the Lord is God.

The People Praise God (1 Kings 18:39)

Jonah

The story of Jonah teaches us a great deal about God's patience and willingness to forgive. Although Jonah was a prophet of God, he blatantly disobeyed God's will both in deed and spirit. Instead of going to Nineveh, he fled in the opposite direction. Later he rebelled against God's compassion for the Ninevites, who were enemies of Israel. Despite Jonah's rebellious spirit, open disobedience, and angry attitude, God forgave him—just as he forgave the Ninevites and just as he'll forgive those who turn to him today.

As soon as young children hear the name Jonah, they want to hear about the big fish that swallowed him. But this is much more than a fish story! The 5- and 6-year-olds in your class take their mistakes to heart. They tend to internalize the problems around them, thinking that family problems are their fault. They often worry that their friends and parents won't love them if they're not perfect. It's important for young children to learn that everyone makes mistakes. During this module, children will see that Jonah sinned against God and made some big mistakes, but God forgave him. Use these lessons to help children understand that God's love is larger than any sin and that God forgives us when we ask him, no matter how badly we fail.

Five Lessons on Jonah

Time Stretchers

Teach children the following song to the tune of "Frère Jacques." (This song is not recorded on the *CD.*) Sing each line and have the children echo it back to you. For extra fun, add the motions.

Where was Jonah? (*Shield eyes and look around.*)
Where was Jonah?
He ran away. (*Run in place.*)
He ran away.
Jumped aboard a big ship. (*Jump.*)
Jumped aboard a big ship.
Sailed away. (*Put hands together and move them back and forth.*)
Sailed away.

Where was Jonah? (*Shield eyes and look around.*)
Where was Jonah?
Asleep down below. (*Lay head on hands.*)
Asleep down below.
Then God sent a big storm. (*Make waves with both hands.*)
Then God sent a big storm.
The wind did blow! (*Cup hands around mouth and blow.*)
The wind did blow!

Where was Jonah? (*Shield eyes and look around.*)
Where was Jonah?
In the sea. (*Make swimming motions.*)
In the sea.
He said, "This storm is my fault." (*Point to self.*)
He said, "This storm is my fault."
"Get rid of me." (*Point thumb away.*)
"Get rid of me."

Where was Jonah? (*Shield eyes and look around.*)
Where was Jonah?
In a big fish. (*Make big circle with arms, palms together, fingers pointing forward.*)
In a big fish.
He prayed and said, "I'm sorry." (*Fold hands and look up.*)
He prayed and said, "I'm sorry."
"I'll do what you wish." (*Nod head.*)
"I'll do what you wish."

Where was Jonah? (*Shield eyes and look around.*)
Where was Jonah?
On the beach. (*Point to the ground.*)
On the beach.
God told the fish to spit him out. (*Touch mouth, then point forward.*)
God told the fish to spit him out.
Then he went to preach. (*Open and close "talking" hands.*)
Then he went to preach.

Jonah Hide-and-Seek

Photocopy the "Jonah" handout from Lesson 10 on page 154. Cut out the figure and glue it on poster board to make it more durable. Play a game of hide-and-seek using the Jonah figure. Let children take turns hiding the figure while the others hide their eyes. Tell children that Jonah had quite an adventure—he was at home, then in a boat, then in a fish! Talk about how God didn't have to look for Jonah because God always knows where everyone is. Remind children that God knows all about us and is always ready to forgive us, just as he forgave Jonah.

Fish Tag

Choose one child to be the Big Fish or "It." Use the center of the room as the sea and pick two opposite walls to be the shores. Have the Big Fish "swim" in the sea while the other children try to swim from one shore to the other without being tagged. Have the Big Fish start each round by standing in the middle of the sea and chanting, "I'm the Big Fish who swims in the sea. You'll have to swim fast to escape from me." As each child is tagged, he or she becomes another fish in the sea and helps the Big Fish tag others. Continue the game until all children have been tagged. For extra fun, have the "fish" put their hands together and wriggle around in the sea. Explain that God sent a big fish to save Jonah from drowning.

Remembering God's Word

Each four- or five-week module focuses on a key Bible verse. The key verse for this module is "You are forgiving and good, O Lord" (Psalm 86:5a).

This module's key verse will teach children that God loves us all the time and is ready to forgive us, even when we disobey and disappoint him. Have fun using these ideas any time during the lessons on forgiveness.

Forgiveness Fish

Have children line up along one side of the room. Invite children to take turns sharing a time they needed to ask God for forgiveness. After each child has shared, have the rest of the class shout, "Lord, you are kind and forgiving" as that child "swims" to the other side of the room with a freestyle or breast stroke motion. Start the game by telling about a time you asked God for forgiveness. Your willingness to share will help your students feel comfortable sharing their own experiences.

Gone Fishin'

Set out a bowl filled with small fish-shaped crackers. Set an empty bowl beside it. Give each child a drinking straw and invite children to "go fishin'." Have each child step up to the cracker bowl, repeat the Bible verse, then try to "catch" a fish by sucking in on the straw and transferring a fish-shaped cracker to the empty bowl. Let children eat the fish they catch. Mention that people usually catch fish, but that our Bible story tells about a fish that caught a man!

Story Enhancements

Make Bible stories come alive in your classroom by bringing in Bible costumes, setting out sensory items, or creating bulletin boards. When children learn with their five senses as well as with their hearts and minds, lessons come alive and children remember what they've learned. The following ideas will help get you started.

Bulletin Board Idea

Since the story of Jonah is so fast-paced, children may have trouble remembering the sequence of events from week to week. Use this bulletin board to help children keep track of the action. Cover the bottom two thirds of a bulletin board with blue paper to represent the sea. For added fun, use blue cellophane wrap instead of paper. Cover the right portion of the bulletin board with brown paper cut from a grocery sack to represent the land. (See sketch in margin.) Cover the top third with pale blue or white paper to represent the sky.

Lesson 9

● Create interest in each week's lesson by placing a table of sensory items near the door of your classroom. Each week add a new item(s) to the table. For this lesson, bring in several types of toy or model boats. For extra fun, place them in a small dishpan of water. Talk about how people in Bible times traveled in boats that used sails and oars instead of motors.

● Create an Ocean-in-a-Jar. Place sand in the bottom of a jar. Fill the jar half full of water and add a few drops of blue food coloring. Place a small toy boat inside the jar. Keep the jar tightly sealed. Point out how peacefully the boat floats in the water. Save the jar for a demonstration of a stormy sea in Lesson 10.

● Photocopy and cut out the "Boat" handout on page 140. Fold a sheet of brown construction paper in half and trace the boat pattern on it, with the fold at the bottom of the boat. Cut out the boat and attach it to the bulletin board. Children will add small paper fish to the bulletin board this week.

Lesson 10

● For this week's lesson, bring in pictures of storms and a sheet of poster board. Let children take turns holding the ends of the poster board and waving it up and down to make a noise like thunder. Tell children there were often sudden storms on the Mediterranean Sea where Jonah's boat sailed.

● Let children gently shake the Ocean-in-a-Jar from last week's lesson. As the toy boat is tossed about, talk about how big the waves must have looked to Jonah and the sailors during the storm.

● Before class, photocopy and cut out the "Jonah" handout on page 154 and tuck Jonah inside the boat. Children will add paper seaweed to the bulletin board this week.

Lesson 11

● For this week's lesson, set out a variety of sea-related items such as seashells, pictures of fish, starfish, seaweed, and a stuffed or toy whale.

● Bring a can of sardines to class. Make sure everyone is standing close to you when you open it. Talk about what it must have smelled like as Jonah sat inside a fish for three whole days! After children have smelled the sardines, place the can in a sealed container and set it out of the children's reach.

● Photocopy and cut out the "Big Fish" handout on page 168. Fold a sheet of black or gray construction paper in half and trace the fish shape onto it with the fold at the bottom of the fish. Cut out the fish and attach it to the bulletin board. Remove the Jonah figure from the boat and place it inside the fish.

Lesson 12

● For this week's lesson, bring in toy cars and trucks and pictures of large cities. Also bring in a pair of sandals. Explain that the Bible says Nineveh was such a large city that it took three days just to see it all. Talk about how people travel today. Ask children what it would be like to walk around a big city for three whole days, wearing sandals instead of sneakers!

● Bring in pieces of burlap for children to touch. Explain that burlap is like the sackcloth the Ninevites wore to let God know how sorry they were. Talk about how scratchy and uncomfortable clothes made of sackcloth must have felt.

● To add the city of Nineveh to the bulletin board, cut out various-sized strips of newspaper to represent buildings. Tape the newsprint buildings on the land portion of the bulletin board, away from the shoreline. Remove the Jonah figure from inside the fish and place him on the shore.

Lesson 13

● For this week's lesson, set out a an artificial plant branch or vine. Set out modeling dough and invite children to make worm shapes to put next to the plant. Talk about how worms can eat and destroy plants and explain that they'll hear about a worm in the Bible story today.

● Tape or staple the artificial plant branch on the bulletin board near Nineveh. Attach a gummy worm to the plant. Make sure the worm is visible. Remove the Jonah figure from the shore and place it near Nineveh on the bulletin board. When you begin "Hear the Bible Story," place the Jonah figure under the plant.

Wrong Way, Jonah

The Point

🖉 God forgives us when we disobey.

The Bible Basis

Jonah 1:1-3. Jonah runs away

At first glance, the story of Jonah is somewhat confusing. When God commanded Jonah to preach at Nineveh, Jonah promptly headed in the opposite direction. Why would Jonah, a prophet of God, refuse to obey God's command? The explanation comes near the end of the story when Jonah declared his anger toward God. "I knew that you are a gracious and compassionate God," he complained. Clearly, Jonah knew that if he preached redemption to the Ninevites, God might spare them. In his mind they were barbarians, not worthy of God's mercy. But while Jonah complained of God's mercy to the Ninevites, he was perfectly willing to accept God's forgiveness for himself.

The 5- and 6-year-olds in your class may often display a selfish attitude similar to Jonah's. They expect forgiveness for themselves from parents and peers but may not be willing to freely offer it. For example, when Johnny went out to play instead of doing his chores, his parents forgave him and let him have ice cream anyway. That was fine with Johnny. But when his sister broke Johnny's favorite truck, he didn't think she deserved forgiveness from anyone. Young children need to learn that God's love and forgiveness are available to anyone who turns to God in repentance. Use this lesson to help children discover that God forgives us even when we disobey.

Getting the Point

🖉 **God forgives us when we disobey.**

It's important to say The Point just as it's written in each activity. Repeating The Point over and over will help children remember it and apply it to their lives.

Children will
● realize that Jonah disobeyed God by running away,
● learn that they can choose between right and wrong,
● help Pockets understand that God forgives us when we disobey, and
● discover that God wants to forgive everyone.

🖉 **The Point**

This Lesson at a Glance

Before the lesson, collect the necessary items for the activities you plan to use. Refer to the Classroom Supplies and Learning Lab Supplies columns to determine what you'll need. Remember to make photocopies of the "Today I Learned..." handout (p. 141) to send home with your children.

Section	Minutes	What Children Will Do	Classroom Supplies	Learning Lab Supplies
Welcome Time	up to 5	**Welcome!**—Receive name tags and be greeted by the teacher.	"Family Name Tags" hand-outs (p. 29), markers, tape or pins	
Let's Get Started Direct children to one or more of the Let's Get Started activities until everyone arrives.	up to 10	**Option 1: Blown Away**—Use drinking straws to watch paint "run away" in a picture.	Drinking straws, scissors, white paper, tempera paint	
	up to 10	**Option 2: Funny Fish**—Make paper fish to use later in the lesson and to decorate the bulletin board.	Construction paper, markers, scissors	
	up to 10	**Option 3: Build a Boat**—Build a human boat and "sail away" as Jonah did.		
Pick-Up Song	up to 5	**We Will Pick Up**—Sing a song as they pick up toys and gather for Bible-Story Time.	CD player	CD: "We Will Pick Up" (track 2)
Bible-Story Time	up to 5	**Setting the Stage**—Open surprise packages and learn about making choices.	Two paper grocery sacks, ribbon, bows, tape, two empty tin cans, small treats	
	up to 5	**Bible Song and Prayer Time**—Sing a song, bring out the Bible, and pray together.	Bible, construction paper, scissors, basket or box, CD player	CD: "God's Book" (track 3), great fish stamp and ink pad
	up to 10	**Hear the Bible Story**—Use paper fish to help tell the story of Jonah from Jonah 1:1-3.	Bible, CD player, paper fish from Option 2, tape	Group's Fold-Out Learning Mat: Jonah's Adventure, CD: "Jonah's Adventure" (track 15)
	up to 10	**Do the Bible Story**—Play a fun game about making choices.		
Practicing the Point	up to 5	**Can You See Me?**—Help Pockets learn about hiding and forgiveness.	Pockets the Kangaroo, blindfold	
Closing	up to 5	**Hand Holders**—Sing a forgiveness song and affirm each other.	CD player	Fold-Out Learning Mat: Jonah's Adventure, CD: "Runaway Jonah" (track 16)
For Extra Time		For extra-time ideas and supplies, see pages 139.		

God forgives us.

Welcome Time

Welcome! (up to 5 minutes)

- Bend down to make eye contact with children as they arrive.
- Greet each child individually with an enthusiastic smile.
- Thank each child for coming to class today.
- Say: **Today we're going to learn that**  **God forgives us when we disobey.**
- Hand out the "Family" name tags children made in the first lesson and help them attach the name tags to their clothing. If some of the name tags were damaged or if some of the children weren't in class that week, have them make new name tags using the photocopiable handout on page 29.
- Direct children to the Let's Get Started activities you've set up.

● **The Point**

Let's Get Started

Set up one or more of the following activities for children to do as they arrive. After you greet each child, invite him or her to choose an activity.

Circulate among the children to offer help as needed and direct children's conversation toward today's lesson. Ask questions such as "Did you ever need to forgive someone?" or "Why is it important to forgive others?"

☐ OPTION 1: Blown Away (up to 10 minutes)

Before this activity, cut several drinking straws in half. You'll need one straw-half for each child in your class. Set out white paper and tempera paint. Give each child a sheet of paper and a straw-half. Place two or three drops of tempera paint on each sheet of paper. Invite children to make designs by blowing through the straws. Point out how the paint tries to "run away" from the straw. Tell children that today's Bible story is about a man named Jonah who disobeyed God by trying to run away from him. Tell children they'll hear how  God forgives us when we disobey.

● **The Point**

☐ OPTION 2: Funny Fish (up to 10 minutes)

Set out construction paper, scissors, and markers. On the chalkboard, draw an outline of a large fish using the illustration in the margin as a model. If your room doesn't have a chalkboard, draw a fish on a sheet of newsprint and tape it to the wall. Invite children to make their own paper fish. Have each child fold a sheet of construction paper in quarters and draw a fish on it, copying the picture on the board. Using the folded paper, children can cut four fish at a time. Tell children that today they'll hear about Jonah, who tried to hide from God by sailing away on the sea. Explain that even though Jonah disobeyed, God forgave him, just as  God forgives us when we disobey.

● **The Point**

✔ Have children make enough fish for everyone in your class. Each child will need four fish shapes to use during "Hear the Bible Story." If you do not choose Option 2, be sure to make construction paper fish before class.

☐ **OPTION 3: Build a Boat (up to 10 minutes)**

Invite children to build a human boat. Say that today's Bible story is about Jonah, who tried to run away from God by sailing in a boat. Have several children sit together on the floor representing the crew of Jonah's boat. Choose one child to stand up in the middle as Jonah. Then put children in position at the ends of the boat. Have other children join hands and stand from point to point, making the human boat. Tell the "boat" to sway gently back and forth, like a boat slowly sailing under sunny skies. Then change the weather by saying, "The wind is beginning to blow...it's getting stronger and stronger...now waves are washing over the boat...now the wind is starting to calm...now there are just little tiny waves rocking the boat gently." Tell children that Jonah tried to run away from God in a boat, but that God forgave him because 🖲 God forgives us when we disobey.

● **The Point**

When everyone has arrived and you're ready to begin the Bible-Story Time, encourage children to quickly finish what they're doing and get ready to clean up.

Pick-Up Song

We Will Pick Up (up to 5 minutes)

Lead children in singing "We Will Pick Up" (track 2) with the *CD* to the tune of "London Bridge." Encourage the children to sing along as they help clean up the room.

If you want to include the names of all the children in your class, sing the song without the *CD* and repeat the naming section. If you choose to use the *CD*, vary the names you use each week.

Sing 🎵

We will pick up all our toys,
All our toys, all our toys.
We will pick up all our toys
And put them all away.

I see (name) picking up,
Picking up, picking up.
I see (name) picking up
And putting toys away.

(Repeat.)

Bible-Story Time

Setting the Stage (up to 5 minutes)

Tell the children that you'll clap your hands to get their attention. Explain that when you clap, children are to stop what they're doing, raise their hands, and focus on you. Practice this signal a few times. Encourage children to respond quickly so you'll have time for all the fun activities you've planned.

Before class, pick out two paper grocery sacks. In one sack place two empty tin cans. Attach ribbons and bows to the sack. In the other sack place special treats for the children in your class, such as tiny erasers, pencils, or cookies. Crumple this sack a little and add no decorations. Tape both sacks shut.

Say: **Let's play a choosing game. Look at these two surprise sacks. Which one would you like to open? Before you decide, come up and look at them more closely.** Allow children to hold and shake the sacks. **Every day we make choices. Right now you have to choose between these two sacks. Later we'll hear how Jonah had to make a choice, too. When you've chosen a sack, sit down on the floor next to it.** When children are all sitting down, ask:

● **Why did you choose this sack?** (It's pretty; I can hear something big inside; it looks nicer.)

● **Was it hard for you to choose?** (No, because one sack looked nicer than the other; yes, it was hard to make up my mind; yes, because I don't know what's inside.)

Say: **Now we'll see if you made good choices. I know you're excited to see what's inside the sacks. Let's open the pretty one first.** Invite children to help open the sack with the bows. Let everyone see what's inside. Say: **Oh, no! Old tin cans! Choosing this sack turned out to be a bad choice, didn't it? Today in our Bible story we'll hear how Jonah made a bad choice.**

Shall we open the other sack now? It doesn't look very pretty, but let's give it a try. Invite children to help you open the second sack. Let them see what's inside. **Wow! Treats for everyone! This sack was a good choice, wasn't it? Let's all share these treats.** Distribute the treats to everyone. Then ask:

● **What made it hard to know which sack to choose?** (We didn't know which one was better; I couldn't tell what was inside.)

Say: **Sometimes it's hard to make choices because we can't see what's going to happen. But God can see everything and will help us make the right choices. Let's find out about Jonah, who made a wrong choice and disobeyed God. Then we'll see that God forgave Jonah because 🖊 God forgives us when we disobey.**

🖊 The Point

Bible Song and Prayer Time (up to 5 minutes)

Before class, make surprise cards for this activity by cutting construction paper into 2×6-inch slips. Prepare a surprise card for each child plus a few extras for visitors. Fold the cards in half, then stamp the *great fish stamp* inside one of the surprise cards. Mark Jonah 1:1-3 in the Bible you'll be using.

Have children sit in a circle. Say: **Now it's time to choose a Bible person to bring me the Bible marked with today's Bible story. As we sing our Bible song, I'll pass out the surprise cards. Don't look inside your card until the song is over.**

Lead children in singing "God's Book" (track 3) with the *CD* to the tune of "Old MacDonald Had a Farm." As you sing, pass out the surprise cards. If you want to include the names of all the children in your class, sing "God's Book" without the *CD*. If you choose to use the *CD*, vary the names you use each week.

Sing

Now it's time to read God's Book
And hear a Bible story.
It's fun to be here with my friends
And hear a Bible story.

(Name)**'s here.**
(Name)**'s here.**
Here is (name).
Here is (name).
Now it's time to read God's Book
And hear a Bible story.

Now it's time to read God's Book
And hear a Bible story.
It's fun to be here with my friends
And hear a Bible story.

(Name)**'s here.**
(Name)**'s here.**
Here is (name).
Here is (name).
Now it's time to read God's Book
And hear a Bible story.

After the song, say: **You may look inside your surprise cards. The person who has the great fish stamped inside his or her card will be our Bible person for today.**

Identify the Bible person, then have the rest of the children clap for him or her. Ask the Bible person to bring you the Bible. Help the Bible person open the Bible to the marked place and show the children where your story comes from. Then have the Bible person sit down.

● **The Point**

Say: (Name) **was our special Bible person today. Each week, we'll have only one Bible person, but each one of you is a special part of our class! Today we're all learning that** ● **God forgives us when we disobey.**

Let's say a special prayer now and ask God to help us learn about his forgiveness. I'll pass around this basket. When the basket comes to you, put your surprise card in it and say, "God, please teach me that you forgive me when I disobey."

Pass around the basket or box. When you've collected everyone's surprise card, set the basket aside and pick up the Bible. Lead children in this prayer: **God, thank you for the Bible and all the stories in it. Teach us today that** ● **you forgive us when we disobey. In Jesus' name we pray, amen.**

● **The Point**

Hear the Bible Story (up to 10 minutes)

Bring out *Group's Fold-Out Learning Mat: Jonah's Adventure.* Have children sit with you on the floor around the folded mat. Hold up the Bible. Say: **Our Bible story comes from the book of Jonah in the Bible.** Hold up the *Fold-Out Mat.* **Our Fold-Out Mat shows us pictures of our Bible story. We'll open our Fold-Out Mat as we listen to the story each week.** Unfold the *Fold-Out Mat* once to show Jonah standing on the shore listening to God. Play

God forgives us.

the "Jonah's Adventure" segment (track 15) on the *CD*. Pause the CD player at the sound of the chime.

Say: **Nineveh was a big city in Bible times.** Ask:

● **Why do you think Jonah didn't want to go there?** (He was scared; the people were bad.)

Say: **Jonah had to make a choice. He had to decide whether or not to obey God.** Give each child four paper fish made in Option 2. Say: **Help me unfold our mat again to find out what Jonah decided to do. Listen for the name Jonah. Every time you hear the name Jonah, toss a fish onto the sea on the *Fold-Out Mat.*** Unfold the *Fold-Out Mat* again and play the rest of the "Jonah's Adventure" segment on the *CD*.

After the story is finished, say: **It sounds like Jonah decided not to obey God.** Ask:

● **What did Jonah do when God told him to go to Nineveh?** (He ran away; he said no; he got on a boat.) Say: **That's right. Jonah disobeyed. He tried to run away and hide from God.** Ask:

● **Do you think anyone can really hide from God? Why or why not?** (No, because God knows where we are; no, because God can always see us.)

Say: **God loves us and watches over us all the time. He knew when Jonah disobeyed, and he knows when we do something wrong. But even when we disobey, God still loves us and wants to forgive us.** Ask:

● **Have you ever forgiven someone?** Let children share a time they've forgiven a friend or family member.

Say: **God wants us to forgive each other, just as he forgives us. It's important to remember that 🖊 God forgives us when we disobey, just as he forgave Jonah when he ran away on the boat. Let's pick up our paper fish and tape them to the water on the bulletin board.** After children have taped up their fish, say: **Let's play a fun game about obeying.**

● **The Point**

Do the Bible Story (up to 10 minutes)

Ask children to help you put chairs against the wall to clear an open space for this activity. Say: **We're going to play a game where you get to decide whether to obey or not. It's a lot like Simon Says, but we'll call it Jonah Says. I'll be Jonah and I'll call out things for you to do. If you choose to obey, do what I say. If you choose not to obey, say, "No, no, never, never, uh, uh, uh!" Then sit down on the floor until you hear me say something you'd like to obey.**

Call out the following commands, preceded by "Jonah Says":

● **Close your eyes and spin around five times without bumping into anyone.**

● **Make a fish face and swim around the room.**

● **Give three people a "high five."**

● **Sing "Jesus Loves Me" in Russian.**

● **Skip backwards around the room.**

● **Hook arms with a partner, then do six jumping jacks together using only your outside arms.**

● **Say the alphabet backwards.**

● **Say "huffy hippopotamuses" five times as fast as you can.**

● **Give two people a backwards hug.**

When the game is finished, ask children to sit in a semicircle around you. Say: **That was a fun game about making choices. Every time I told you what to do, you had to decide whether or not to obey. We all have to make choices every day.** Ask:

● **What made you decide to obey or disobey my commands?** (I did them if I thought it would be fun; I couldn't do some of them even if I tried; I didn't do the ones that were too hard.)

● **How was making choices in the game like making choices every day?** (You still had to make a decision; sometimes you feel like obeying and sometimes you don't; sometimes I don't want to do things that are hard.)

● **How was it different?** (The game wasn't real; in the game it didn't really matter what I decided; I wouldn't get in trouble if I decided not to obey in the game.)

● **What are some hard choices you make every day?** (Whether to mind my parents or not; whether to share my toys; whether to do my chores when I don't want to.)

Say: **Sometimes our choices are simple, like what color shirt to wear. But sometimes our choices are harder, like whether to obey our parents or teachers. We all have to decide between right and wrong. From time to time, we all make bad choices. Sometimes we even disobey on purpose like Jonah did. When we do the wrong thing on purpose, that's called sin. But even when we disobey, we can go to God and say we're sorry, because if we ask him ✎ God forgives us when we disobey.**

I wonder if Pockets ever disobeys. Let's call her and find out. Pockets! Oh, Pockets! Are you coming to see us today?

● **The Point**

Practicing the Point

Can You See Me? (up to 5 minutes)

Before class, put a blindfold over Pockets' eyes.

Bring out Pockets the Kangaroo and go through the following puppet script. When you finish the script, put Pockets away and out of sight.

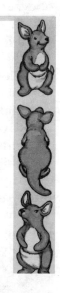

Where's Pockets

PUPPET SCRIPT

Pockets: *(Comes in with a blindfold over her eyes.)* Hi, everybody.

Teacher: Hi, Pockets.

Pockets: Can you see me?

Teacher: Can you see her, class? *(Let children respond.)*

Pockets: *(Peeks out with one eye.)* Now can you see me?

Teacher: Can you see her, class? *(Let children respond.)*

Pockets: *(Covers that eye and peeks out with the other eye.)* <u>Now</u> can you see me?

(Continued)

God forgives us.

Teacher: I can, Pockets. Can you, class? *(Let children respond.)*

Pockets: *(Turns her back toward the class.)* <u>Now</u> can you see me?

Teacher: What do you think, class? *(Let children respond.)*

Pockets: *(Turns toward class and removes blindfold.)* I don't get it! How did you know where I was when I was hiding?

Teacher: You thought you were hiding, but we could still see you, Pockets. Today we heard a Bible story about a man named Jonah who disobeyed God and then tried to hide.

Pockets: Really? Did he use a blindfold?

Teacher: No, he didn't. Class, can you tell Pockets how Jonah tried to hide from God? *(Encourage children to tell how God told Jonah to preach at Nineveh, but how he disobeyed and ran away from God. Discuss how Jonah sailed away on a boat, trying to hide from God.)*

Pockets: Wow! Was God really, really mad at Jonah?

Teacher: No, God still loved Jonah. Jonah learned that 🖊 God forgives us when we disobey. Next week we'll hear how God helped Jonah learn about forgiveness.

Pockets: Boy! I can't wait. See you then. 'Bye, everyone. *(Have children say goodbye.)*

● **The Point**

TODAY I LEARNED . . .

We believe that Christian education extends beyond the classroom into the home. Photocopy the "Today I Learned..." handout (p. 141) for this week and send it home with your children. Encourage parents to use the handout to plan meaningful family activities to reinforce this week's topic. Follow up the "Today I Learned..." activities next week by asking children what their families did.

Closing

Hand Holders (up to 5 minutes)

Have children stand in a circle around the *Fold-Out Mat.* Say: **We've all been learning that** 🖊 **God forgives us when we disobey. Let's learn a song about forgiveness.** Lead children in acting out and singing "Runaway Jonah" (track 16) with the *CD* to the tune of "London Bridge."

● **The Point**

Sing

Jonah runs and hides from God. *(Hands covering face.)*
Where is he? *(Hand shielding eyes.)*
Can you see? *(Hand shielding eyes.)*

Jonah runs and hides from God *(hands covering face)*,
But God forgives him. *(Hands over heart.)*

In the belly of a fish *(holding nose)*,
Jonah prays *(praying hands)*,
Three whole days. *(Praying hands.)*
In the belly of a fish *(holding nose)*,
And God forgives him. *(Hands over heart.)*

◔ The Point

Have children sit on the floor around the *Fold-Out Mat.* Say: **Isn't it great that ◔ God forgives us when we disobey? Can you think of a time when you disobeyed? You don't have to tell anyone. Just pretend you're holding that time in your hand. Now get with a friend and hold hands. See how your friend's hand covers up your own? That's how God's forgiveness covers up the bad things we do. When we're sorry for wrong things we do and ask God to forgive us, he will. Let's thank God for his forgiveness right now.**

Pray: **Dear God, thank you for loving us even when we make bad choices. Thank you for being willing to forgive us when we disobey. In Jesus' name we pray, amen.**

God forgives us.

For Extra Time

If you have a long class time or want to add additional elements to your lesson, try one of the following activities.

LIVELY LEARNING: Run Away Game

Before this activity, remove the *pretend rock* from the Learning Lab.

Remind children that God forgave Jonah because  God forgives us when we disobey. Have children stand in a circle with their hands behind their backs like fish tails. Pick someone to be "It." It will carry the *pretend rock* around the outside of the circle while all the children say, "Jonah, Jonah, disobeyed. God forgave him anyway." At the end of the phrase, It will put the *pretend rock* into another child's hands, and that child will chase It around the circle. Have both children take giant steps instead of running, as they try to return to the open spot in the circle. If It gets back to the open spot in the circle without being tagged, the child holding the *pretend rock* will be It.

● The Point

MAKE TO TAKE: Boat Trip

Before class, photocopy the "Boat" handout from page 140. You'll need one handout for each child in your class. Set out the handouts, paper plates, scissors, tape, crayons, paper fasteners, and the *great fish stamp and ink pad.* Explain that everyone will make a boat that rocks back and forth in a paper-plate "sea." Show children how to cut a paper plate in half then cut the straight edges in a zigzag pattern to create "waves." Help children tape the curved edges of their paper plates together. Then show them how to cut out the square, fold it into a boat, and secure the boat between the waves with a paper fastener. Demonstrate how the boat rocks back and forth in the waves. Let children use the *great fish stamp* and crayons to decorate their paper plates. Remind them Jonah tried to run from God by sailing away in a boat but that God forgave Jonah because  God forgives us when we disobey.

● The Point

TREAT TO EAT: Orange Boats

Before class, cut several oranges in half. You'll need one orange half for each child in your class. Set out orange halves and a bag of triangular corn chips. Form three groups: the Boat Handlers, the Sail Makers, and the Sail Setters. Have children work in assembly line fashion, with the Boat Handlers lining up the orange halves, the Sail Makers taking out and lining up the corn chips, and the Sail Setters inserting a chip in the center of each orange half. As children work, remind them that Jonah sailed away on a boat when he ran away from God.

STORY PICTURE: Jonah Runs Away

Give each child a photocopy of the "Today I Learned..." handout from page 141. Set out cotton balls, glue sticks, watercolor paints, paint brushes, and the *great fish stamp and ink pad.* Invite children to use the stamp to decorate their pictures then use watercolors to paint the water. Have children stretch and glue cotton balls on their pictures as clouds.

God forgives us.

Boat

Photocopy this page, then cut the large square on the solid lines.

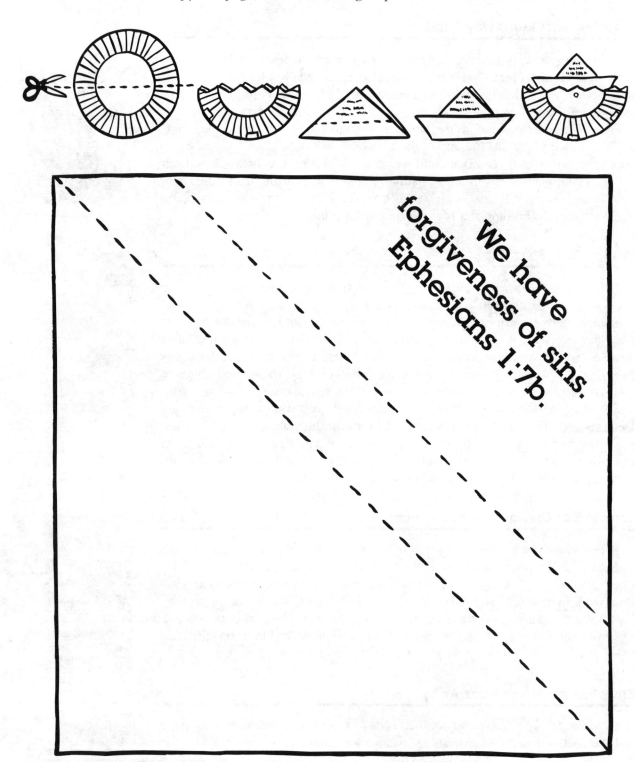

We have forgiveness of sins.
Ephesians 1:7b.

God forgives us.

TODAY I LEARNED...

The Point 🖉 God forgives us when we disobey.

LESSON 9

Today your child learned that God forgives us when we disobey. Children learned that Jonah disobeyed God, but God forgave Jonah when he prayed. They talked about making good and bad choices and about how important it is to obey God.

Verse to Learn

"You are forgiving and good, O Lord" (Psalm 86:5a).

Ask Me...

● Why did Jonah run away from God?
● Did you ever feel like running away instead of obeying?
● When is a time you obeyed God even when it was hard?

Family Fun

● Make a Family Forgiveness Flower for family members to share this week. Cut 15 to 20 petals from tissue paper, pinch the base of each petal, and tape petals to a drinking-straw stem. Place the Forgiveness Flower in a prominent place in your home. When someone offers or asks for forgiveness this week, pick a petal and hand it to the person who's being forgiven.

Jonah Runs Away (Jonah 1:1-3)

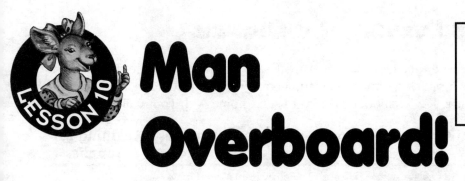

Man Overboard!

The Point

✐ God forgives us when we cause trouble.

The Bible Basis

Jonah 1:4-17. Jonah is thrown overboard.

As the storm raged, Jonah lay asleep below deck. Perhaps he felt secure in thinking the further he got from Joppa, the further he got from God. Above, the terrified sailors were throwing cargo overboard, praying to their gods, and trying to row for shore. When they confronted Jonah, he realized that his disobedience might cost not only his own life, but the life of every sailor on that boat. He convinced the crew to throw him overboard. When they did, the waters became calm. After seeing this awesome demonstration of power, the crew worshiped God. And Jonah, who expected to die, was rescued by a great fish and went on to preach redemption to an entire city.

There's no denying that young children can cause trouble. The 5- and 6-year-olds in your class are energetic, inquisitive, and impulsive. For them, pushing boundaries is a normal part of growing up. They may openly defy and disobey those in authority. Kindergartners often find themselves in trouble because they fail to think ahead and anticipate the consequences of their actions. Children need to learn that the wrong choices they make affect others, but that God is patient and forgiving. Use this lesson to reassure children that God will forgive them, even when they cause trouble.

Getting the Point

✐ **God forgives us when we cause trouble.**

It's important to say The Point just as it's written in each activity. Repeating The Point over and over will help the children remember it and apply it to their lives.

Children will
- learn that God forgives us even when we cause trouble,
- realize that we can cause trouble for others if we disobey,
- help Pockets learn to forgive, and
- understand that God takes care of us even if we cause trouble.

✐ **The Point**

This Lesson at a Glance

Before the lesson, collect the necessary items for the activities you plan to use. Refer to the Classroom Supplies and Learning Lab Supplies columns to determine what you'll need. Remember to make photocopies of the "Today I Learned..." handout (p. 155) to send home with your children.

Section	Minutes	What Children Will Do	Classroom Supplies	Learning Lab Supplies
Welcome Time	up to 5	**Welcome!**—Receive name tags and be greeted by the teacher.	"Family Name Tags" handouts (p. 29), markers, pins or tape	
Let's Get Started Direct children to one or more of the Let's Get Started activities until everyone arrives.	up to 10	**Option 1: Tunnel Fish**—Drape plastic trash bags over an aisle of chairs to make a large fish to crawl through.	Large trash bags, chairs, tape, construction paper, scissors, markers	
	up to 10	**Option 2: Stormy Sounds**—Record their own tape of storm sound effects.	Cassette player, blank tape, poster board, plastic milk jug, water	
	up to 10	**Option 3: Seaweed Squiggles**—Make their own paper seaweed.	Construction paper, scissors, tape	
Pick-Up Song	up to 5	**We Will Pick Up**—Sing a song as they pick up toys and gather for Bible-Story Time.	CD player	CD: "We Will Pick Up" (track 2)
Bible-Story Time	up to 5	**Setting the Stage**—Use shadows to learn God is with them.	Flashlight	
	up to 5	**Bible Song and Prayer Time**—Sing a song, bring out the Bible, and pray together.	Bible, construction paper, scissors, basket or box, CD player	CD: "God's Book" (track 3), great fish stamp and ink pad
	up to 10	**Hear the Bible Story**—Pretend they're in a storm as they hear the Bible story.	Bible, CD player, fan, bowl of water, module bulletin board, "Jonah" handout (p. 154)	*Fold-Out Learning Mat: Jonah's Adventure*, CD: "Jonah's Adventure" (track 17), great fish stamp and ink pad, fish squirter
	up to 10	**Do the Bible Story**—Use a pretend boat to re-enact the Bible story.	Rope, tunnel fish from Option 1, cassette tape from Option 2, cassette player	Great fish stamp and ink pad
Practicing the Point	up to 5	**Baby-Bottle Blues**—Help Pockets learn to forgive.	Pockets the Kangaroo, plastic baby bottle	
Closing	up to 5	**Fish From God**—Sing a song about God's forgiveness.	CD player	CD: "Runaway Jonah" (track 16)
For Extra Time	For extra-time ideas and supplies, see page 153.			

God forgives us.

Welcome Time

Welcome! (up to 5 minutes)

- Bend down to make eye contact with children as they arrive.
- Greet each child individually with an enthusiastic smile.
- Thank each child for coming to class today.
- As children arrive, ask them about last week's "Today I Learned..." discussion. Ask questions such as "Can you tell a way you obeyed God last week?" and "Did you forgive anyone last week?"
- Say: **Today we're going to learn that**  **God forgives us when we cause trouble.**
- Hand out the "Family" name tags children made in Lesson 1 and help them attach the name tags to their clothing. If some of the name tags were damaged or if some of the children weren't in the class that week, have them make new name tags using the photocopiable patterns on page 29.
- Direct the children to the Let's Get Started activities you've set up.

● **The Point**

Let's Get Started

Set up one or more of the following activities for children to do as they arrive. After you greet each child, invite him or her to choose an activity.

Circulate among children to offer help as needed and direct children's conversation toward today's lesson. Ask questions such as "What troubles have you been in?" or "Who helped you with your troubles?"

OPTION 1: Tunnel Fish (up to 10 minutes)

Before class, cut open three or four large plastic trash bags. Black bags would work best. Set out construction paper, scissors, and tape. Tell children you're going to build a big fish, like the one in the story of Jonah. In a corner of the room, have children help you arrange two rows of three or four chairs facing outward, with enough space between the rows for children to crawl through. Stretch trash bags across the rows of chairs, forming a tunnel effect. Tape the bags to the chairs. Let children cut out and tape white construction paper teeth to the front of the fish. If you wish, have them add construction paper scales to the sides of the fish. Explain that they'll get a chance to use the fish today and in coming lessons as they learn more about Jonah. Tell children today they'll hear how God sent a big fish to save Jonah during a storm, and that while he was in the fish, Jonah learned that ● God forgives us when we cause trouble.

● **The Point**

✔ You'll use the tunnel fish several times during this module. If you don't choose this Option, make a simpler fish before class by draping a large blanket over a table or two rows of chairs. Plan to leave the fish in place for the rest of the module.

Option 2: Stormy Sounds (up to 10 minutes)

The Point 🖊

You'll need an empty plastic milk jug, one-third full of water; a sheet of poster board; and a cassette recorder with a blank tape. Tell children that today they'll hear how God sent a big storm to surround Jonah's boat. Tell children that Jonah caused trouble for the sailors on the boat. But God took care of Jonah during the storm, because 🖊 God forgives us when we cause trouble. Invite children to record their own storm sound effects. Encourage them to make whooshing wind noises and to drum their fingertips on a table to make rain sounds. For thunder, have them wave the sheet of poster board back and forth. For crashing waves, let them shake the milk jug. As children experiment with their sound effects, ask questions such as "Have you ever sailed in a boat?" and "How do you think Jonah felt when a big storm came along?" Make the tape three to five minutes long. You'll use it in "Do the Bible Story."

Option 3: Seaweed Squiggles (up to 10 minutes)

The Point 🖊

Set out scissors, tape, and brown and green construction paper. Invite children to make "seaweed" to add to the bulletin board by cutting thin strips of paper and crumpling them. Let them tape their seaweed strips to the bottom of the sea on the bulletin board. Tell them today they'll hear how Jonah caused a lot of trouble for the sailors on his boat because God sent a big storm when Jonah tried to run away. But God forgave Jonah because 🖊 God forgives us when we cause trouble.

When everyone has arrived and you're ready to move on to the Bible-Story Time, encourage the children to finish what they're doing and get ready to clean up.

Pick-Up Song

We Will Pick Up (up to 5 minutes)

Lead children in singing "We Will Pick Up" (track 2) with the *CD* to the tune of "London Bridge." Encourage children to sing along as they help clean up the room.

If you want to include the names of all the children in your class, sing "We Will Pick Up" without the *CD* and repeat the naming section. If you choose to use the *CD*, vary the names you use each week.

Sing 🎵

We will pick up all our toys,	I see (name) picking up,
All our toys, all our toys.	Picking up, picking up.
We will pick up all our toys	I see (name) picking up
And put them all away.	And putting toys away.
	(Repeat.)

God forgives us.

Bible-Story Time

Setting the Stage (up to 5 minutes)

Tell the children you'll clap your hands to get their attention. Explain that when you clap, the children are to stop what they're doing, raise their hands, and focus on you. Practice this signal a few times. Encourage children to respond quickly so you'll have time for all the fun activities you've planned.

For this activity, plan to go to a room without windows or cover the windows in your classroom. It isn't necessary for the room to be completely dark. Have children stand in front of a blank wall. Say: **Let's play a fun shadow game. Let's see if we can make our shadows jump, skip, and hop.**

Using a powerful flashlight, allow children to make shadows against the wall. As children play with their shadows, ask:

● **What happens if you try to run away from your shadow?** (It stays with me; it goes wherever I go; I can't run away from it.)

After children have played with their shadows for two or three minutes, turn on the lights and ask children to sit in a circle on the floor. Ask:

● **What did you learn about your shadow?** (That it does everything I do; that I couldn't get away from it; that you can't run away from your shadow.)

Say: **Even when you tried, you couldn't hide from your shadows. They were always with you. God is always with you, too. He's with you when it's dark and when it's light and all the time. And just as we couldn't hide from our shadows, we can't hide from God. God can always see us.** Ask:

● **Why do you think God watches us all the time?** (To see if we do something wrong; because he loves us.)

Say: **God watches over us all the time because he loves us. He watches over us to keep us safe and to help us make good choices. But even when we get in trouble, God still loves us.** Ask:

● **How do you usually feel after you've done something wrong?** (Bad; sorry; scared.)

● **What makes you feel better when you've done something wrong?** (When I say I'm sorry; when my parents say it's OK.)

Say: **If we're sorry and we ask God to forgive us, he will, because God forgives us when we cause trouble. In our Bible story today, we'll hear how Jonah caused trouble for himself and all the sailors on his boat. Let's get ready for our Bible song; then we'll find out more about Jonah.**

● The Point

Bible Song and Prayer Time (up to 5 minutes)

Before class, make surprise cards for this activity by cutting construction paper in 2×6-inch slips. Prepare a surprise card for each child, plus a few extras for visitors. Fold the cards in half, then stamp the *great fish stamp* inside one of the surprise cards. Mark Jonah 1:4-17 in the Bible you'll be using.

Have the children sit in a circle. Say: **Now it's time to choose a Bible person to bring me the Bible marked with today's Bible story. As we sing our Bible song, I'll pass out the surprise cards. Don't look inside your card until the song is over.**

Lead children in singing "God's Book" (track 3) with the *CD* to the tune of "Old MacDonald Had a Farm." As you sing, pass out the folded surprise cards. If you want to include the names of all the children in your class, sing the song without the *CD* and repeat the naming section. If you choose to use the *CD*, vary the names you use each week.

Sing

Now it's time to read God's Book
And hear a Bible story.
It's fun to be here with my
    friends
And hear a Bible story.

(Name)'s here.
(Name)'s here.
Here is (name).
Here is (name).
Now it's time to read God's Book
And hear a Bible story.

Now it's time to read God's Book
And hear a Bible story.
It's fun to be here with my
    friends
And hear a Bible story.

(Name)'s here.
(Name)'s here.
Here is (name).
Here is (name).
Now it's time to read God's Book
And hear a Bible story.

After the song, say: **You may look inside your surprise cards. The person who has the great fish stamped inside his or her card will be our Bible person for today.**

Identify the Bible person, then have the rest of the children clap for him or her. Ask the Bible person to bring you the Bible. Help the Bible person open the Bible to the marked place and show the children where your story comes from. Then have the Bible person sit down.

Say: (Name) **was our special Bible person today. Each week, we'll have only one Bible person, but each one of you is a special part of our class!**

The Point

Today we're all learning that ⬛ **God forgives us when we cause trouble.**

Let's say a special prayer now and ask God to help us learn how he forgives us. I'll pass around this basket. When the basket comes to you, put your surprise card in it and say, "God, please teach me that you forgive me when I cause trouble."

Pass around the basket or box. When you've collected everyone's surprise card, set the basket aside and pick up the Bible. Lead children in this prayer: **God, thank you for the Bible and all the stories in it. Teach us today that**

The Point

⬛ **you forgive us when we cause trouble. In Jesus' name we pray, amen.**

Hear the Bible Story (up to 10 minutes)

Before class, be sure you have put the Jonah figure inside the boat on the bulletin board. You'll find bulletin board directions in the Module Introduction on page 126.

Before this activity, set the *great fish stamp and ink pad* near the bulletin board. Also set out a portable fan, a bowl of water, and the *fish squirter* from the *Learning Lab*.

Bring out the Bible, the *Fold-Out Learning Mat: Jonah's Adventure,* and the *CD.* Set the closed *Fold-Out Mat* on the floor and have children sit around it. Hold up the Bible. Say: **Our Bible story today comes from the**

God forgives us.

book of Jonah in the Bible. Hold up the *Fold-Out Mat.* Say: **Our *Fold-Out Mat* shows us pictures of our Bible story. Let's use the pictures to review last week's Bible story.**

Unfold the *Fold-Out Mat* once to the picture showing Jonah on the shore listening to God. Say: **I'm going to ask some questions about last week's lesson. If you know the answers, put your pointer finger on your nose. I'll call on someone to give the answer.** Ask:

● **Where did God tell Jonah to go?** (To Nineveh; to a big city.)

● **Why didn't Jonah want to go to Nineveh?** (He didn't like the people there; the people there were bad.)

● **What did Jonah do when God told him to go to Nineveh?** (He disobeyed; he ran away; he hopped on a boat.)

Unfold the *Fold-Out Mat* once more to the picture of Jonah on the boat looking back toward Joppa.

Say: **Let's look over at our bulletin board.** Ask:

● **Where is Jonah on the bulletin board?** (In the boat; I don't see him.)

Say: **I'll give you a clue. He's hiding somewhere on the bulletin board. I'll go over to the board and use the *great fish stamp* to find him. Every time I stamp the board, you tell me if I'm getting close or not. If I'm getting close to Jonah, clap your hands; if I'm far away from Jonah, don't clap.**

Go to the bulletin board. As children respond, make a trail with the *great fish stamp* to Jonah's hiding place inside the boat. When the children guess correctly, lift the outer flap of the boat to reveal Jonah hiding inside. Say: **There's Jonah! We couldn't see him hiding inside the boat, but God could! Now let's find out what happened to Jonah on the boat.**

Rejoin the children at the *Fold-Out Mat.* Say: **Today we're going to hear about a big storm that God sent while Jonah was on the boat.** Ask:

● **Has anyone here ever been in a really bad, scary storm?** (Yes.)

● **What was it like?** (It was windy; there was thunder and lightning; the lights went out.)

Say: **That's right. Storms usually have lots of rain and wind. I'm going to make a pretend storm while you listen to the story!** Open the *Fold-Out Mat* once more to the picture of Jonah on the boat during the storm. Turn on the fan. For added fun, dip the mouth of the *fish squirter* in the water and squeeze to draw in some water. Then gently spray the children with water as they listen to the story. Play the "Jonah's Adventure" segment (track 17) on the *CD,* unfolding the *Fold-Out Mat* each time you hear the chime.

Stop the *CD* at the end of the segment and turn off the fan. Say: **Wow! What an exciting story!** Ask:

● **Why do you think God sent that storm?** (Because Jonah had been bad; to show Jonah he was watching; to show Jonah he couldn't hide.)

● **How do you think Jonah felt when he knew the storm was his fault?** (Scared; worried; sorry he had disobeyed.)

Say: **Jonah didn't just get himself in trouble—he caused a lot of trouble for the sailors on the boat, too.** Ask:

● **What could've happened to the sailors on the boat with Jonah?** (They could've lost their boat and drowned.)

● **Can you share a time when you or someone you know caused trouble for other people?** (Once my neighbor started a fire in her garage; once my brother got in a fight at school.)

God forgives us.

Say: **Even though Jonah got himself in trouble, God was watching during the storm and took care of everyone on the boat. Even when the sailors threw Jonah overboard, God was still watching.** Ask:

● **Why did God send the big fish?** (To swallow Jonah; to save Jonah from drowning.)

● **The Point**

Say: **Jonah caused trouble, but God still loved him. That's why he sent the big fish to save Jonah. We all cause trouble sometimes, just like Jonah. It's important to remember that ● God forgives us when we cause trouble. No matter what we do, God loves us and wants to forgive us.**

Now let's play a stormy game to help us remember today's Bible story.

Do the Bible Story (up to 10 minutes)

Before this activity, bring a rope long enough to make a large circle on the floor and tie the ends of the rope together. The circle will have to be big enough for all the children in your class to stand inside.

Have children sit in a group on the floor and lay the circle of rope on the floor nearby. If you chose Option 2, set out the cassette player and sound effects tape you made. Set the *great fish stamp and ink pad* near the tunnel fish you made in Option 1.

Say: **Pretend you're on the boat with Jonah. Step inside the circle on the floor and pick up the rope. The rope will be the edge of our boat. Hold on while you pretend you're in a storm. Pretend the boat is tossing on the waves; move the rope from side to side and up and down.**

If you made the sound-effects tape in Option 2, say: **I'll play the storm sounds we taped earlier.** Prompt the children to pretend their boat is in a big storm. Make comments such as "The boat's going up really high, and down really low" and "Look out, here comes a big wave!" After a few moments of storm play, ask:

● **Why did the sailors throw Jonah overboard?** (Because Jonah told them that would stop the storm; because they were afraid and wanted the storm to stop.)

Say: **Now pretend you're going overboard like Jonah. Put the rope on the floor and hop overboard. Get down on the floor and pretend you're swimming.** Make comments such as "Jonah must have been really scared when he was in the water" and "Jonah couldn't save himself, only God could save Jonah." After a few moments of swimming, ask:

● **What happened to Jonah after he got dumped in the sea?** (He got swallowed by a huge fish.)

Say: **Right! He was swallowed by a giant fish. Swim over to the tunnel fish and crawl through one by one. When you come out the other side, I'll stamp your hands.**

After you've stamped each child's hand with the *great fish stamp,* say: **The stamp on your hands will remind you that just as God forgave Jonah, ● God forgives us when we cause trouble. I wonder if Pockets has ever been in trouble. Do you think she has?**

● **The Point**

Practicing the Point

Baby-Bottle Blues (up to 5 minutes)

Before class, put a small plastic baby bottle in Pockets' pouch.

Have children sit in a circle. Take out Pockets the Kangaroo and go through the following script. When you finish the script, put Pockets away and out of sight.

Baby-Bottle Blues

PUPPET SCRIPT

Pockets: *(With plastic baby bottle in her pouch)* Hello, everyone.

Teacher: Hi! What do you have in your pocket, Pockets?

Pockets: It's a baby bottle—for my sister!

Teacher: Why are you giving her a bottle?

Pockets: 'Cause she's a big baby, that's why! She's learning how to drink from a cup, and she's supposed to stay in the kitchen. But she spilled grape juice all over my bedspread! My brand new bedspread! She's such a big baby; she's always causing trouble!

Teacher: But Pockets, she didn't mean to spill. Didn't you ever make a mess when you were a little kangaroo?

Pockets: No! I was <u>ahl-ways</u> a lady!

Teacher: I bet if we asked your parents, they might remember a few messes you made. Maybe you don't remember them because your parents forgave you right away. Can't you forgive your little sister?

Pockets: No! She's always causing trouble, and I won't forgive her!

Teacher: You know, today we heard more about Jonah. He caused trouble, but God forgave him.

Pockets: Did he spill his juice?

Teacher: Oh, something much worse, Pockets. He disobeyed God. Class, why don't you tell Pockets about Jonah and all the trouble Jonah caused? *(Encourage children to tell Pockets how Jonah disobeyed God, how he caused trouble for the sailors when God sent the storm, and how God sent a fish to save Jonah from drowning.)*

Pockets: Wow! *(Pause.)* Jonah really did cause trouble! And God still forgave him?

Teacher: Yes, Pockets, ✎ God forgives us when we cause trouble.

Pockets: *(Looks at baby bottle for a moment, then speaks softly.)* I guess if God can forgive, maybe I should, too. Do you think I should forgive my sister? *(Let class respond.)*

(Continued)

● **The Point**

God forgives us.

Pockets: Thanks for helping me forgive. I'm sure I'll feel a lot better. I'm gonna take this baby bottle home and see if my sister wants to play dolls with me. 'Bye, everybody.
(Have children say goodbye.)

TODAY I LEARNED . . .

We believe that Christian education extends beyond the classroom into the home. Photocopy the "Today I Learned . . ." handout (p. 155) for this week and send it home with your children. Encourage parents to use the handout to plan meaningful family activities to reinforce this week's topic. Follow up the "Today I Learned . . ." activities next week by asking children what their families did.

Closing

The Point

Fish From God (up to 5 minutes)

Form a circle around the tunnel fish. Ask: **What did you learn today?** (That God saved Jonah; that God forgives us when we cause trouble.)

Say: **Give everyone a high five to show how glad we are that God saved Jonah and that God forgives us when we cause trouble.**

Have everyone pat the fish. Then lead children in singing and acting out "Runaway Jonah" (track 16) to the tune of "London Bridge."

Sing

Jonah runs and hides from God. *(Hands covering face.)*
Where is he? *(Hand shielding eyes.)*
Can you see? *(Hand shielding eyes.)*
Jonah runs and hides from God *(hands covering face)*,
But God forgives him. *(Hands over heart.)*

In the belly of a fish *(holding nose)*,
Jonah prays *(praying hands)*,
Three whole days. *(Praying hands.)*
In the belly of a fish *(holding nose)*,
And God forgives him. *(Hands over heart.)*

Say: **Before we go, let's hold hands around the fish and thank God for his forgiveness.**

Pray: **Dear God, thank you for forgiving us, even when we cause trouble. In Jesus' name we pray, amen.**

God forgives us.

For Extra Time

If you have a long class time or want to add additional elements to your lesson, try one of the following activities.

LIVELY LEARNING: Fish Rib Game

Play a London Bridge fish game. Have two children stand facing each other with arms forming an arch of "fish ribs." Say: **As we sing our song, we'll walk under the fish ribs. At the end of each verse, the fish ribs will come down and catch whoever is under the arch. If you're caught, go inside our big fish and count to three. Then come out and join the fish ribs in trying to catch other people.** Sing the following song to the tune of "London Bridge" without the CD.

Jonah runs and hides from God.	In the belly of a fish,
Where is he?	Jonah prays,
Can you see?	Three whole days.
Jonah runs and hides from God,	In the belly of a fish,
But God forgives him.	And God forgives him.

Remind children that even though Jonah caused trouble, God forgave him because 🐟 God forgives us when we cause trouble.

● **The Point**

MAKE TO TAKE: The Big Fish

Before this activity, gather one bath-tissue tube for each child in your class. Set out tubes, construction paper, glue, and scissors. Invite children to make their own tunnel fish to take home. Let them cut construction paper scales, fins, and teeth to glue on the tube. Remind children that God sent the big fish to save Jonah because 🐟 God forgives us when we cause trouble.

● **The Point**

TREAT TO EAT: Stormy Seas

Let children make their own stormy-sea treats. Set out cold milk, plastic spoons, small paper cups, a box of instant pudding, a bag of small gummy fish or gummy worms, and a jar with a tight-fitting lid. Following package directions, mix pudding and milk in the jar. Stir slightly. Let children each add a gummy fish or worm to the "sea" in the jar. Tightly close the lid. Let each child have a turn shaking the jar to make waves. When pudding has thickened, spoon it into paper cups. As children enjoy their snacks, talk about how God forgave Jonah because 🐟 God forgives us when we cause trouble.

● **The Point**

STORY PICTURE: Jonah Is Thrown Into the Sea

Set out cotton balls, crayons, markers, glue sticks, and *great fish stamp and ink pad.* Show children how to make their pictures look stormy by drawing zigzag lightning bolts and darkening the cotton balls with markers and gluing them to the sky. Let them share the *great fish stamp and ink pad* to add fish to the sea. Remind children that just as he forgave Jonah, 🐟 God forgives us when we cause trouble.

● **The Point**

God forgives us.

Jonah

Photocopy the handout. Cut out the figure of Jonah.

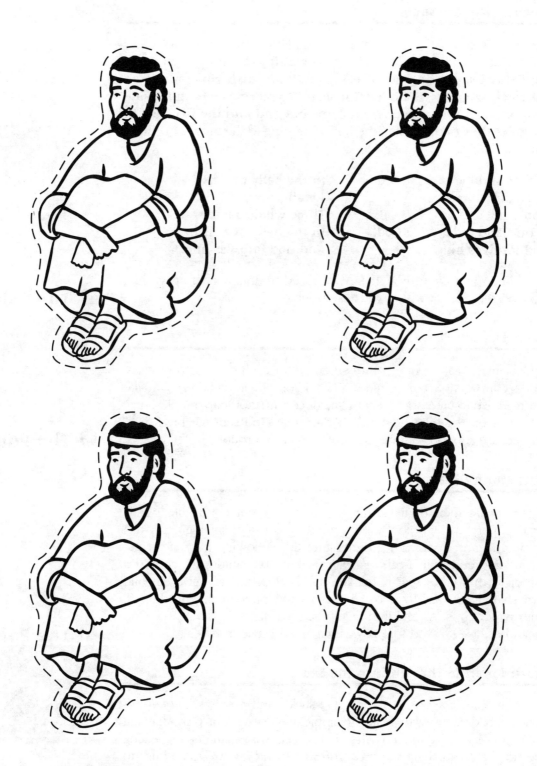

God forgives us.

TODAY I LEARNED...

The Point ✏ God forgives us when we cause trouble.

LESSON 10

Today your child learned that God forgives us when we cause trouble. Children learned that God forgave Jonah and sent the big fish to save Jonah's life. They talked about making mistakes and forgiving others, even when they cause trouble.

Verse to Learn

"You are forgiving and good, O Lord" (Psalm 86:5a).

Ask Me...

● Why did God send the fish to Jonah?
● Why is it important to forgive each other?
● Can you tell about a time someone forgave you?

Family Fun

● Obtain a large box from a local appliance store and make a big fish to play with at home. Make it a family project to build, decorate, and "feed" the fish! If it's nice weather, let the fish live outside in the yard for a few days. Encourage your child to share the story of Jonah with neighborhood friends who come by to play in the fish.

Jonah Is Thrown Overboard (Jonah 1:4-17)

God Forgives Jonah

The Bible Basis

Jonah 2:1-10. Jonah prays inside the fish.

Although the fish saved his life, Jonah couldn't have been very comfortable sitting in its belly for three days. But we don't hear any complaints! Jonah realized that God had provided the fish to save his life and marveled at the miracle. He described the fear he felt as he sank deeper and deeper into the sea. When his "life was ebbing away," Jonah remembered to pray. And there's the crux of this lesson. Jonah wasn't forgiven and released from the fish until he prayed. When we're sorry for something we've done, God wants us to pray for forgiveness. He'll grant it, just as he did for Jonah.

The 5- and 6-year-olds in your class can easily understand the need to pray for forgiveness. Stacy knows not to throw a ball in the house. But she breaks the rule and her mother's favorite vase. She feels terrible until she knows her mother has forgiven her and has been reassured of her mother's love. Stacy needs to know that God forgives completely and that God's love for us is never shaken. Even young children can begin to sense the peace that comes with knowing that God wipes the slate clean every time he forgives. But we have to ask. We have to pray. Use this lesson to teach children that it doesn't matter where we pray—on the school bus or in a fish—God will forgive us when we pray to him.

Getting the Point

🖊 **God forgives us when we pray to him.**

It's important to say The Point just as it's written in each activity. Repeating The Point over and over will help the children remember it and apply it to their lives.

Children will
- learn that God hears their prayers,
- understand how important it is to talk to God,
- learn that God forgives us when we ask, and
- help Pockets understand that we can pray anywhere.

🖊 **The Point**

This Lesson at a Glance

Before the lesson, collect the necessary items for the activities you plan to use. Refer to the Classroom Supplies and Learning Lab Supplies columns to determine what you'll need. Remember to make photocopies of the "Today I Learned..." handout (p. 168) to send home with your children.

Section	Minutes	What Children Will Do	Classroom Supplies	Learning Lab Supplies
Welcome Time	up to 5	**Welcome!**—Receive name tags and be greeted by the teacher.	"Family Name Tags" handouts (p. 29), markers, pins or tape	
Let's Get Started Direct children to one or more of the Let's Get Started activities until everyone arrives.	up to 10	**Option 1: Feed the Fish**—Play a fun game to feed the tunnel fish they made.	Tunnel fish made in Lesson 10, scraps of paper	
	up to 10	**Option 2: Praying Places**—Play a guessing game to think about different places they can pray.		
	up to 10	**Option 3: Prayer Spyglasses**—Make spyglasses to look for different places to pray.	Cardboard towel tubes, blue cellophane, scissors, tape	
Pick-Up Song	up to 5	**We Will Pick Up**—Sing a song as they pick up toys and gather for Bible-Story Time.	CD player	CD: "We Will Pick Up" (track 2)
Bible-Story Time	up to 5	**Setting the Stage**—Hide under a blanket to see how Jonah might have felt inside the fish.	Blanket(s)	
	up to 5	**Bible Song and Prayer Time**—Sing a song, bring out the Bible, and pray together.	Bible, construction paper, scissors, basket or box, CD player	CD: "God's Book" (track 3), great fish stamp and ink pad
	up to 10	**Hear the Bible Story**—Sit squished "inside" a fish as they hear today's story.	Bible, masking tape, CD player, module bulletin board, "Big Fish" handout (p. 167)	Fold-Out Learning Mat: Jonah's Adventure, CD: "Jonah's Adventure" (track 18)
	up to 10	**Do the Bible Story**—Play a fun game about different places to pray, then sing a song.	CD player	CD: "I'll Pray" (track 19)
Practicing the Point	up to 5	**Pray Today!**—Help Pockets understand that we can pray anywhere.	Pockets the Kangaroo	
Closing	up to 5	**Private Prayer**—Have private prayer time inside the tunnel fish.	Tunnel Fish made in Lesson 10	
For Extra Time		For extra-time ideas and supplies, see page 166.		

God forgives us.

Welcome Time

Welcome! (up to 5 minutes)

- Bend down to make eye contact with children as they arrive.
- Greet each child individually with an enthusiastic smile.
- Thank each child for coming to class today.
- As children arrive, ask them about last week's "Today I Learned..." discussion. Ask questions such as "Did anyone you know cause trouble last week?" and "Did you forgive them?"
- Say: **Today we're going to learn that ◐ God forgives us when we pray to him.**
- Hand out the "Family" name tags children made in Lesson 1 and help them attach the name tags to their clothing. If some of the name tags were damaged or if some of the children weren't in class that week, have them make new name tags using the photocopiable patterns on page 29.
- Direct the children to the Let's Get Started activities you've set up.

◐ **The Point**

Let's Get Started

Set up one or more of the following activities for children to do as they arrive. After you greet each child, invite him or her to choose an activity.

Circulate among children to offer help as needed and direct children's conversation toward today's lesson. Ask questions such as "When do you pray?" or "What do you do when you're sorry for something you've done?"

▢ OPTION 1: Feed the Fish (up to 10 minutes)

Set out a supply of scrap paper. Invite children to make paper wads from the scraps. Have children line up with their paper wads in front of the tunnel fish you made last week. Tell children they'll be "feeding" the fish by tossing paper wads into the fish's mouth. The first child in line will be the Leader and will determine how to toss the paper wads, such as underhand, over the shoulder, or under a leg. Each child will toss a paper wad following the Leader's method. If a child misses the fish's mouth, he or she must sit inside the fish until that round is finished. When every child in line has fed the fish, have children collect the paper wads, line up, and begin the game again. Make sure every child has a chance to be the Leader and encourage each Leader to choose a new way to toss the paper wads. Ask questions such as "Who sent the fish to swallow Jonah?" and "Why did God send the fish?" Tell children that today's Bible story is about how Jonah learned that ◐ God forgives us when we pray to him.

◐ **The Point**

▢ OPTION 2: Praying Places (up to 10 minutes)

Invite children to play a guessing game about places to pray. Have children sit in a circle. Choose one child to silently think of a place we can pray.

That child will say, "I'm thinking of a place to pray." The other children in the circle will try to guess the place by asking questions that can only be answered by saying "yes" or "no." Let children take turns thinking of praying places to guess. Encourage them to think of the many different places we can pray, such as in church, in bed, at school, or on the bus. Tell children that today they'll learn how God heard Jonah pray—even when Jonah was in the belly of a fish! Jonah prayed for forgiveness, and God heard him. Jonah

🖊 **The Point**   learned that God forgives us when we pray to him.

☐ OPTION 3: Prayer Spyglasses (up to 10 minutes)

Before class, collect several empty cardboard bath-tissue or paper-towel tubes. Cut a 2-inch length of tube for each child in your class. Also cut blue cellophane into 3×3-inch squares, one for each child. Set out tissue tubes, scissors, tape, and cellophane squares. Invite children to make Prayer Spyglasses. Help them each tape a cellophane square over one end of the tube. Invite children to look around the room through their spyglasses, thinking of different places

🖊 **The Point**   to pray. Talk about how Jonah prayed, even from inside a fish. And when Jonah prayed, God listened. Jonah learned that 🖊 God forgives us when we pray to him.

> ✔ If you don't have blue cellophane, have children use blue markers to color squares of clear plastic wrap. You can also substitute rolled poster board for paper-towel tubes.

When everyone has arrived and you're ready to move on to the Bible-Story Time, encourage the children to finish what they're doing and get ready to clean up.

Pick-Up Song

We Will Pick Up (up to 5 minutes)

Lead children in singing "We Will Pick Up" (track 2) with the *CD*, to the tune of "London Bridge." Encourage the children to sing along as they help clean up the room.

If you want to include the names of all the children in your class, sing "We Will Pick Up" without the *CD*. If you choose to use the *CD*, vary the names you use each week.

Sing 🎵

We will pick up all our toys,	I see (name) picking up,
All our toys, all our toys.	Picking up, picking up.
We will pick up all our toys	I see (name) picking up
And put them all away.	And putting toys away.

(Repeat.)

God forgives us.

Bible-Story Time

Setting the Stage (up to 5 minutes)

Tell the children you'll clap your hands to get their attention. Explain that when you clap, the children are to stop what they're doing, raise their hands, and focus on you. Practice this signal a few times. Encourage children to respond quickly so you'll have time for all the fun activities you've planned.

Bring enough blankets to cover yourself and all the children in your class as you sit in a group. Say: **Let's play Be in the Belly! We'll sit together on the floor, and I'll cover us with this blanket.** When everyone is covered, ask:

- **What's it like under here?** (Dark; hot; fun.)
- **Do you think you'd like to sit under here for three days?** (No.)

Say: **Even though I can't see all of you under the blanket, I can still hear you. Just like when Jonah was in the fish, God could still hear him. When Jonah prayed, God answered.** Remove the blanket.

Ask:

- **How was being under the blanket a little like being inside the fish?** (It was dark; it was a little scary; I didn't know what was going to happen.)
- **How was it different?** (This was just pretend; it wasn't smelly; we weren't alone.)

Say: **When we were under the blanket, we weren't alone—we were all together. Jonah was inside the fish by himself, but he wasn't alone either. God was with Jonah and heard him when he prayed. Let's get ready for our Bible-Story Time. That would be a good place for us to pray, and we can find out more about Jonah, too.**

Bible Song and Prayer Time (up to 5 minutes)

Before class, make surprise cards for this activity by cutting construction paper in 2×6-inch slips. Prepare a surprise card for each child plus a few extras for visitors. Fold the cards in half, then stamp the *great fish stamp* inside one of the surprise cards. Mark Jonah 2:1-10 in the Bible you'll be using.

Have children sit in a circle. Say: **Now it's time to choose a Bible person to bring me the Bible marked with today's Bible story. As we sing our Bible song, I'll pass out the surprise cards. Don't look inside your card until the song is over.**

Lead children in singing "God's Book" (track 3) with the *CD* to the tune of "Old MacDonald Had a Farm." As you sing, pass out the surprise cards. If you want to include the names of all the children in your class, sing "God's Book" without the *CD*. If you choose to use the *CD*, vary the names you use each week.

Sing

Now it's time to read God's Book	(Name)'s here.
And hear a Bible story.	(Name)'s here.
It's fun to be here with my friends	Here is (name).
And hear a Bible story.	Here is (name).
	Now it's time to read God's Book
	And hear a Bible story.

Now it's time to read God's Book	(Name)'s here.
And hear a Bible story.	(Name)'s here.
It's fun to be here with my	Here is (name).
friends	Here is (name).
And hear a Bible story.	Now it's time to read God's Book
	And hear a Bible story.

After the song, say: **You may look inside your surprise cards. The person who has the great fish stamped inside his or her card will be our Bible person for today.**

Identify the Bible person, then have the rest of the children clap for him or her. Ask the Bible person to bring you the Bible. Help the Bible person to open the Bible to the marked place and show the children where your story comes from. Then have the Bible person sit down.

Say: (Name) **was our special Bible person today. Each week we'll have only one Bible person, but each of you is a special part of our class! Today we're all learning that 🖊 God forgives us when we pray to him.**

🖊 The Point

Let's say a special prayer now and ask God to teach us that he forgives us when we pray. I'll pass around this basket. When the basket comes to you, put your surprise card in it and say, "God, thank you for listening when we pray."

Pass around the basket or box. When you've collected everyone's surprise card, set the basket aside and pick up the Bible. Lead children in this prayer: **God, thank you for the Bible and all the stories in it. Teach us today that 🖊 you forgive us when we pray to you. In Jesus' name we pray, amen.**

🖊 The Point

Hear the Bible Story (up to 10 minutes)

Before class, be sure you have added the "Big Fish" handout to the bulletin board and put the Jonah figure inside the fish. You'll find bulletin board directions in the Module Introduction on page 127.

Before this activity, use masking tape to make a fish shape or circle on the floor. Make the shape big enough so all the children in your class can sit "squished" inside. Set out the *Fold-Out Learning Mat: Jonah's Adventure.*

Say: **Let's use the bulletin board to review our Jonah story.** Ask:

● **Who can tell me where we left Jonah last time?** (Inside the fish.) Show children Jonah tucked inside the fish on the bulletin board.

Say: **Today we'll find out what Jonah did inside the fish. Let's sit on the floor around our *Fold-Out Mat* and get ready for today's story.**

Have children help you unfold the *Fold-Out Mat* six times to the picture of Jonah inside the fish. Review the story as you unfold the book. Ask:

● **Why was Jonah running away from God?** (He didn't want to go to Nineveh; he didn't want to obey God.) Say: **Pretend you're Jonah running away. Take big, long giant steps and go around the room as fast as you can.** Then have children sit down again around the *Fold-Out Mat*. Say: **Whew! Running away is hard work!** Ask:

● **What happened to Jonah's boat?** (It got caught in a storm; it was tossed up and down on the waves; God didn't let it sink.)

● **Why did God send the storm?** (Because Jonah was bad; to show Jonah God knew where Jonah was; so Jonah would obey.) Say: **Stand up and**

pretend you're being blown about by the wind of a giant storm. Then have children sit down and ask:

● **How did Jonah wind up in the belly of a fish?** (God sent a big storm; the sailors threw Jonah overboard to stop the storm.) Say: **Hold your nose with one hand, say "P-U!" and give each other high fives with the other hand.** Then ask:

● **Why did God send the fish to swallow Jonah?** (To save him; to keep him from drowning.)

Say: **You all did a great job of remembering. As we listen to our story today, I want you to sit squished in the fish's tummy.** Have children sit within the tape outline on the floor. **It's kind of a tight fit and may not be very comfortable. But that's how Jonah must have felt, too. You know, it must have smelled pretty bad inside that fish. Why don't you hold your nose as you listen to the story? Listen for the part where Jonah starts praying. When you hear how Jonah prayed inside the fish, stop holding your nose and make praying hands.** Play the "Jonah's Adventure" segment (track 18) on the *CD,* unfolding the *Fold-Out Learning Mat* when you hear the chime.

Stop the *CD* at the end of the segment. Say: **That was great! You really listened well. Jonah must have been happy to get out of that fish. Pretend you're being spit out of your fish onto dry land.** Encourage children to jump outside the tape outline and pretend to lie on the shore breathing fresh air again. Then ask them to sit around the *Fold-Out Learning Mat.*

Say: **When the sailors tossed Jonah overboard, he thought he was going to drown! But in the water he remembered to pray, and God sent the fish to save him. All of a sudden, Jonah found himself in a fish belly.** Ask:

● **Why do you think God let Jonah spend three whole days inside the fish?** (To teach him a lesson; to make him sorry; to show him who was boss.)

● **What do you suppose Jonah said to God?** (He said he was sorry; he thanked God for saving him; he asked God to let him out.)

● **What do you say to God when you're sorry for something you've done?** (I'm sorry; forgive me; I won't do it again.)

Say: **Jonah thanked God for saving his life, and said he was sorry he had disobeyed. He asked God to forgive him, and God did. Just as God forgave Jonah,** ✏ **God forgives us when we pray to him. When God forgave Jonah, he told the fish to spit Jonah out onto dry land. Our *Fold-Out Learning Mat* says the fish may have hiccuped Jonah out onto dry land. Let's play a fun hiccup game.**

✏ **The Point**

Do the Bible Story (up to 10 minutes)

Say: **Today we've been talking about different places to pray. We learned that Jonah even prayed in the belly of a fish. I'll name some different places to pray. If you've ever prayed in the place I name, hop up as if you were in a fish and it had a big hiccup. Ready? Here we go!** Have children squat in a circle. Then repeat the following statements, letting children respond with hiccups after each one.

● **I can pray anywhere; I pray in bed.**
● **I can pray anywhere; I pray at dinner.**

- I can pray anywhere; I pray at school.
- I can pray anywhere; I pray in the car.
- I can pray anywhere; I pray at church.
- I can pray anywhere; I pray in my yard.
- I can pray anywhere; I pray on a hilltop.
- I can pray anywhere; I pray in a tent.
- I can pray anywhere; I pray on a lake.

The Point

Say: **That was fun! God hears us when we pray, and** **God forgives us when we pray to him. Let's sing a song to remind us to always pray to God.** Sing "I'll Pray" (track 19) with the *CD* to the tune of "Jesus Loves Me."

Sing

God wants me to always pray;
No matter what the people say.
God will answer all my cares,
When I offer him my prayers.
Yes, God, I'll pray.
Yes, God, I'll pray.
Yes, God, I'll pray.
I'll pray to only you.

Say: **That was a good song about praying. You know, I wonder if Pockets remembers to pray. Let's ask her.** Encourage children to call Pockets.

Practicing the Point

Pray Today (up to 5 minutes)

Have the children sit in a circle. Take out Pockets the Kangaroo. Go through the following script. When you finish the script, put Pockets out of sight.

Pray Today

PUPPET SCRIPT

Pockets: *(Bouncing and bopping around)* Hi, everyone! How are you today? It's great to see you!

Teacher: Good morning, Pockets. My, you seem happy today.

Pockets: *(Hugging herself)* Ooh, I AM happy. I really, really am.

Teacher: That's wonderful, Pockets. Do you want to share with us why you're so happy?

Pockets: Sure! I got forgiven today! I had to wait all week, but I finally got forgiven!

Teacher: What do you mean, Pockets? Why did you have to wait?

(Continued)

Pockets: *(Looking down)* Well, I did something bad last Monday. I broke my sister's doll and hid it in the closet. I told her I was sorry that night, but I had to wait until church today to ask God to forgive me. *(Looking happy)* And now he did.

Teacher: Pockets, you didn't have to wait all week. You could have prayed for forgiveness right away.

Pockets: Are you sure? I thought I could only pray in church.

Teacher: No. In fact, today we heard how Jonah prayed in a very strange place. Class, why don't you tell Pockets about Jonah praying for forgiveness? *(Encourage children to tell about Jonah praying in the fish and how God forgave him.)*

Pockets: Wow! Jonah prayed in the belly of a fish?

Teacher: Yes. We can pray for forgiveness any time, anywhere.

Pockets: And God still hears us? And the prayers still count?

Teacher: Class, what do you think? *(Let children respond.)*

Pockets: Well! I wasted all week feeling bad! I could have been forgiven on Monday! I'll remember that no matter when or where, ✏ God forgives us when we pray to him. I'm going to go home and make sure my parents know about this. 'Bye, and thanks for telling me.
(Have children say goodbye.)

● **The Point**

TODAY I LEARNED...

We believe that Christian education extends beyond the classroom into the home. Photocopy the "Today I Learned..." handout (p. 168) for this week and send it home with your children. Encourage parents to use the handout to plan meaningful family activities to reinforce this week's topic. Follow up the "Today I Learned..." activities next week by asking children what their families did.

Closing

Private Prayer (up to 5 minutes)

Have the class stand and hold hands around the tunnel fish. Say: **We're each going to take turns praying inside our big fish. Crawl in the front of the fish and say something like, "Dear God, thank you for listening when I pray." After you pray, come out the back and let the next person go in. The rest of us will stand quietly around the fish. I'll pray first.**

Spend only a moment inside the fish. Then stand near the back of the fish and move the circle forward so the next person in line is directly in front of the fish. When everyone has had a turn, close with a group prayer.

Pray: **Dear God, thank you for teaching us that ✏ you forgive us when we pray to you. In Jesus' name we pray, amen.**

● **The Point**

For Extra Time

If you have a long class time or want to add additional elements to your lesson, try one of the following activities.

LIVELY LEARNING: Rock Bop

Have children stand in a circle. Toss the *pretend rock* gently in the air and have the children try to keep it in the air by bopping it to one another. Tell children to pretend their feet are cemented to the floor so they can't move. If the rock falls to the ground, the person it lands closest to must name a place he or she can pray. Then that person can bop the rock to start the game again. Remind children that ● God forgives us when we pray to him.

● **The Point**

MAKE TO TAKE: Jonah Prays

Before class, cut sheets of transparency film into quarters. You'll need one quarter sheet for each child in your class. Make photocopies of the "Jonah" handout from page 154 and the "Big Fish" handout from page 167 for every child in your class. Set out crayons, permanent markers, and tape. Encourage children to color and cut out the Jonah and fish pictures. Show children how to sandwich the transparency film between the fish and Jonah pictures (fish on top, then film, then Jonah.) Secure the layers on top with tape.

Demonstrate how to use a permanent marker to draw ribs on the transparency to look like Jonah's in "jail" in the fish's tummy. When the fish and transparency layers are lifted, Jonah is "free." Talk about how Jonah prayed for forgiveness and God set him free. Tell children Jonah learned that ● God forgives us when we pray to him.

● **The Point**

TREAT TO EAT: Fish Rib Crackers

Set out graham crackers, peanut butter, string licorice, plastic knives, and scissors. Form three groups: the Cracker Snappers, the Super Spreaders, and the Careful Cutters. The Cracker Snappers will gently snap the graham crackers in half. The Super Spreaders will use plastic knives to spread peanut butter on the crackers. The Careful Cutters will use scissors to cut short lengths of licorice and place them on the crackers to look like fish ribs. As children enjoy their snacks, discuss how Jonah prayed for forgiveness while he was inside the fish. Remind them that ● God forgives us when we pray to him.

> **Note:**
> Before preparing the snacks, make sure children are not allergic to the ingredients.

● **The Point**

STORY PICTURE: Something's Fishy!

Hand each child a photocopy of the "Today I Learned..." handout from page 168. Set out markers, glue sticks, and scraps of paper. Allow children to color their pictures. Have them tear paper scraps into small pieces and glue them on the fish to look like scales.

Big Fish

Photocopy the handout. Cut out the fish picture.

God forgives us.

TODAY I LEARNED...

The Point 🖊 God forgives us when we pray to him.

Today your child learned that God forgives us when we pray to him. Children learned that God forgave Jonah when he prayed inside the fish. They discussed why it's important to talk to God in prayer.

Verse to Learn

"You are forgiving and good, O Lord" (Psalm 86:5a).

Ask Me...

● What do you think it was like to be inside a fish for three days?

● When do you like to pray?

● When is a time God answered our prayers?

Family Fun

● Have a Pick-a-Prayer Party. Put all family members' names in a hat. Have each person draw out a name and pray especially for that person for the rest of the week. Have everyone talk to the person he or she is praying for to find out about that person's needs or concerns.

● Visit a pet shop or aquarium and guess how big Jonah's fish must have been. Talk about how God sent the fish at that special moment to save Jonah's life. Discuss how God is in control of all of nature.

Jonah Prays Inside the Fish (Jonah 2:1–10)

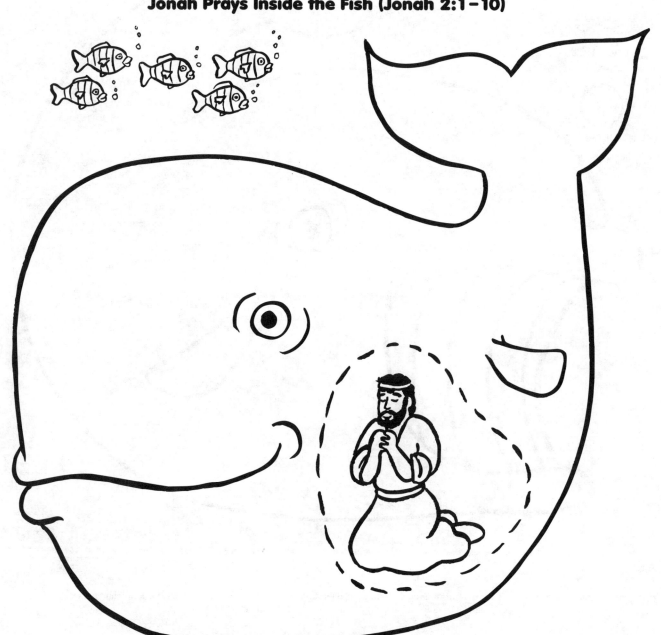

Oh So Sorry

The Point

🖊 God forgives us when we're sorry for what we've done.

The Bible Basis

Jonah 3:1-10. Jonah preaches in Nineveh.

After the fish delivered Jonah safely onto the beach, God again gave the command to go to Nineveh. This time the prophet obeyed. Jonah invaded the prosperous city proclaiming God's impending destruction. The people of Nineveh immediately took Jonah's message to heart. They wore sackcloth and fasted to show their repentant spirit. The king decreed that no man or animal should eat or drink. He commanded the people to turn from evil and pray to God for forgiveness. God heard their prayers and graciously granted them a reprieve. God gave them another chance, just as he had given Jonah.

The kindergartners in your class frequently find themselves embroiled in squabbles that result from selfish choices. Parents and other caregivers may coax a reluctant "I'm sorry" from a quarreling child. But more often, that child will say anything just to get out of an uncomfortable situation and get on with the fun things at hand. The children in your class are old enough to understand that God knows what's in their hearts and that true repentance involves a purposeful change in behavior. Use this lesson to teach children that when we tell God we're sorry—and really mean it—God always forgives us.

Getting the Point

🖊 **God forgives us when we're sorry for what we've done.**

It's important to say The Point just as it's written in each activity. Repeating The Point over and over will help the children remember it and apply it to their lives.

Children will
● learn that God wants to forgive them,
● hear how Jonah finally gave God's message to the people of Nineveh,
● help Pockets learn about God's true forgiveness, and
● discover they need to tell God they're sorry when they do something wrong.

🖊 **The Point**

This Lesson at a Glance

Before the lesson, collect the necessary items for the activities you plan to use. Refer to the Classroom Supplies and Learning Lab Supplies columns to determine what you'll need. Remember to make photocopies of the "Today I Learned..." handout (p. 180) to send home with your children.

Section	Minutes	What Children Will Do	Classroom Supplies	Learning Lab Supplies
Welcome Time	up to 5	**Welcome!**—Receive name tags and be greeted by the teacher.	"Family Name Tags" handouts (p. 29), markers, pins or tape	
Let's Get Started Direct children to one or more of the Let's Get Started activities until everyone arrives.	up to 10	**Option 1: Second Chance Glance**—Play a memory game and get a second chance to look at items they've forgotten.	Assortment of small classroom items, tray, newsprint	Fish squirter, great fish stamp
	up to 10	**Option 2: Fish-Squirter Paintings**—Make paintings with the fish squirter.	Thinned tempera paint, bowls, paper, cotton swabs, newspapers	Fish squirter
	up to 10	**Option 3: Again and Again**—Make fish stamps on paper.	Paper, stamps, and ink pads	Great fish stamp and ink pad
Pick-Up Song	up to 5	**We Will Pick Up**—Sing a song as they pick up toys and gather for Bible-Story Time.	CD player	CD: "We Will Pick Up" (track 2)
Bible-Story Time	up to 5	**Setting the Stage**—Have several chances to feed the tunnel fish.	Tunnel fish from Lesson 10, scrap paper	
	up to 5	**Bible Song and Prayer Time**—Sing a song, bring out the Bible, and pray together.	Bible, construction paper, scissors, basket or box, CD player	CD: "God's Book" (track 3), great fish stamp and ink pad
	up to 10	**Hear the Bible Story**—Use a snack to help tell the story.	Bible, goldfish crackers, CD player, module bulletin board	Fold-Out Learning Mat: Jonah's Adventure, CD: "Jonah's Adventure" (track 20)
	up to 10	**Do the Bible Story**—Travel a pretend Path to Forgiveness and learn how the Ninevites asked for forgiveness.	Paper plates	Great fish stamp and ink pad, cape
Practicing the Point	up to 5	**Sorry Sackcloth**—Help Pockets understand God's forgiveness.	Pockets the Kangaroo, paper sack	
Closing	up to 5	**Sorry From the Heart**—Sing a song and pray together.	CD player	CD: "The Forgiveness Song" (track 21)
For Extra Time		For extra-time ideas and supplies, see page 179.		

God forgives us.

Welcome Time

Welcome! (up to 5 minutes)

- Bend down to make eye contact with children as they arrive.
- Greet each child individually with an enthusiastic smile.
- Thank each child for coming to class today.
- As children arrive, ask them about last week's "Today I Learned..." discussion. Ask questions such as "Where were you when you prayed last week?" and "What did your family pray about?"
- Say: **Today we're going to learn that** 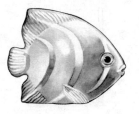 **God forgives us when we're sorry for what we've done.**
- Hand out the "Family" name tags children made in Lesson 1 and help them attach the name tags to their clothing. If some of the name tags were damaged or if some of the children weren't in class that week, have them make new name tags using the photocopiable patterns on page 29.
- Direct the children to the Let's Get Started activities you've set up.

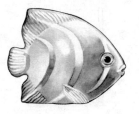
The Point

Let's Get Started

Set up one or more of the following activities for children to do as they arrive. After you greet each child, invite him or her to choose an activity.

Circulate among the children to offer help as needed and direct children's conversation toward today's lesson. Ask questions such as "What do you do when you're sorry for something you've done?" or "How can we show God we're sorry?"

Option 1: Second Chance Glance (up to 10 minutes)

Before class, set aside an assortment of small classroom items such as a pencil, a pair of scissors, a paper clip, a small cup, a roll of tape, a paper fastener, a small Bible, an eraser, a crayon, a marker, the *great fish stamp,* and the *fish squirter.* Place six of the items on a tray and cover the tray with a sheet of newsprint. Ask for a volunteer who will look at the items on the tray then try to name each of the items when you cover them up again. Have the volunteer look at the items for five seconds, then cover them and see how many items the volunteer can name. If the volunteer can't remember all the items, say, "Here—I'll give you a second chance." Uncover the tray and let the volunteer name the items he or she forgot. Then let the volunteer prepare the tray, with six new items for the next player. Each time a player forgets an item, give that child a second chance to look at the tray. Explain that in today's Bible story, God gave Jonah a second chance to obey, just as players in this game got second chances.

Option 2: Fish-Squirter Paintings (up to 10 minutes)

Set out paper, cotton swabs, the *fish squirter,* and two or three small bowls of thinned tempera paint. Cover your work area with a vinyl cloth or newspapers. You may want to have your children put on paint shirts or use large paper grocery bags, cut up the back, with the neck and armholes cut out. Tell children they'll be making "Fish-Squirter Paintings." First the fish will "swallow" the paint, just as the fish in the Bible story swallowed Jonah. Demonstrate how to dip the mouth of the *fish squirter* in the paint and squeeze it to draw in some paint. Then the fish will "spit out" the paint, just as the fish spit out Jonah. Let children take turns using the *fish squirter* to make designs on their papers. While children are waiting to use the squirter, let them paint with cotton swabs. Tell children they'll hear a story of how God forgave Jonah and had the fish spit him out because  God forgives us when we're sorry for what we've done.

● The Point

☐ OPTION 3: Again and Again (up to 10 minutes)

Set out paper, the *great fish stamp and ink pad,* and other stamps and ink pads you may have. Encourage children to see how many times they can make prints after stamping on the ink pad just once. Point out how the prints get lighter each time as the ink runs out. Talk about how God's forgiveness never runs out. Tell children they'll hear how God forgave Jonah and gave him another chance to preach to the people of Nineveh. God forgave the people of Nineveh, too, because  God forgives us when we're sorry for what we've done.

● The Point

When everyone has arrived and you're ready to move on to the Bible-Story Time, encourage the children to finish what they're doing and get ready to clean up.

Pick-Up Song

We Will Pick Up (up to 5 minutes)

Lead children in singing "We Will Pick Up" (track 2) with the *CD* to the tune of "London Bridge." Encourage the children to sing along as they help clean up the room.

If you want to include the names of all the children in your class, sing "We Will Pick Up" without the *CD*. If you choose to use the *CD*, vary the names you use each week.

Sing

We will pick up all our toys,
All our toys, all our toys.
We will pick up all our toys
And put them all away.

I see (name) picking up,
Picking up, picking up.
I see (name) picking up
And putting toys away.

(Repeat.)

God forgives us.

Bible-Story Time

Setting the Stage (up to 5 minutes)

Tell children you'll clap your hands to get their attention. Explain that when you clap, children are to stop what they're doing, raise their hands, and focus on you. Encourage children to respond quickly so you'll have time for all the fun activities you've planned.

Before this activity, set out a stack of scrap paper. Gather children around the tunnel fish made in Lesson 10.

Say: **I think it's time to feed our tunnel fish. He looks pretty hungry to me. We'll crumple up this scrap paper and pretend it's his favorite food.** Have each child crumple up two or three paper scraps then line up as far from the tunnel fish as the room allows.

Say: **Let's try feeding the fish from here. We'll each take a turn trying to throw a paper wad into the fish's mouth.** Let each child take a turn. To those who miss, say: **Maybe we're too far away. We need another chance. Let's get a little closer and try again.** Continue moving closer to the fish until everyone has successfully "fed" it. Then gather children in a group on the floor and ask:

● **How many chances did you get to feed the fish?** (Two; three; four.)

● **When you mess up in real life, is it important to get a second chance? Explain.** (Yes, because it makes you feel better if you get it right the second time; yes, but people don't always give you a second chance.)

● **Does God give people a second chance? Explain.** (Yes, because God forgives us when we mess up; yes, if we pray and tell him we're sorry.)

Say: **Today we're going to hear how God forgave Jonah and gave him another chance to preach in Nineveh. And when the people of Nineveh told God they were sorry, God forgave them, too! They learned that** 🖊 **God forgives us when we're sorry for what we've done. Let's stuff the rest of our paper wads into that hungry fish and get ready for our Bible story.**

🖊 **The Point**

Bible Song and Prayer Time (up to 5 minutes)

Before class, make surprise cards for this activity by cutting construction paper in 2×6-inch slips. Prepare a surprise card for each child plus a few extras for visitors. Fold the cards in half, then stamp the *great fish stamp* inside one of the surprise cards. Mark Jonah 3:1-10 in the Bible you'll be using.

Have the children sit in a circle. Say: **Now it's time to choose a Bible person to bring me the Bible marked with today's Bible story. As we sing our Bible song, I'll pass out the surprise cards. Don't look inside your card until the song is over.**

Lead children in singing "God's Book" (track 3) with the *CD* to the tune of "Old MacDonald Had a Farm." As you sing, pass out the surprise cards. If you want to include the names of all the children in your class, sing "God's Book" without the *CD*. If you choose to use the *CD*, vary the names you use each week.

God forgives us.

Sing

Now it's time to read God's Book
And hear a Bible story.
It's fun to be here with my
    friends
And hear a Bible story.
	Now it's time to read God's Book
	And hear a Bible story.
	It's fun to be here with my
	    friends
	And hear a Bible story.

(Name)'s here. (Name)'s here. Here is (name). Here is (name). Now it's time to read God's Book And hear a Bible story.	(Name)'s here. (Name)'s here. Here is (name). Here is (name). Now it's time to read God's Book And hear a Bible story.

After the song, say: **You may look inside your surprise cards. The person who has the great fish stamped inside his or her card will be our Bible person for today.**

Identify the Bible person, then have the rest of the children clap for him or her. Ask the Bible person to bring you the Bible. Help the Bible person open the Bible to the marked place and show the children where your story comes from. Then have the Bible person sit down.

Say: **(Name) was our special Bible person today. Each week we'll have only one Bible person, but each of you is a special part of our class! Let's say a special prayer now and ask God to help us learn about his forgiveness. I'll pass around this basket. When the basket comes to you, put your surprise card in it and say, "God, teach us to ask for forgiveness when we're sorry for what we've done."**

Pass around the basket or box. When you've collected everyone's surprise card, set the basket aside and pick up the Bible. Lead children in this prayer: **God, thank you for the Bible and all the stories in it. Teach us today that ⬛ you forgive us when we're sorry for what we've done. In Jesus' name we pray, amen.**

⬤ The Point

Hear the Bible Story (up to 10 minutes)

Before class, move the Jonah figure to the shore on the bulletin board. Instructions for the bulletin board this week are in the Module Introduction on page 127.

Have children line up facing the bulletin board. Say: **Today we're going to take a backwards walk through our Bible story. When you think you know the answer to a question, put your hands on your head. Then I'll call on someone. Each time someone answers my question correctly, everyone can take a step backwards.** Ask:

● **Where is Jonah?** (On the beach; on dry land.)

● **How did he get there?** (The fish spit him out.)

● **Why did the fish spit him out?** (God told the fish to spit him out; Jonah was sorry and God forgave him.)

● **How did Jonah get inside the fish?** (The sailors threw him into the sea; God sent the fish to save Jonah from drowning.)

● **Why did the sailors throw Jonah into the sea?** (Because he told them to; so the storm would stop.)

● **Why did God send the storm?** (To stop Jonah from running away; because Jonah disobeyed him.)

● **Why did Jonah run away on a boat?** (Because he didn't want to go to Nineveh and preach.)

● **Why did God want Jonah to go to Nineveh?** (To tell the people to stop sinning; to tell the people they needed to ask God to forgive them.)

Say: **Good job! You've backed all the way through our story and all the way to the back of the room. Now let's hear how God gave Jonah a second chance to obey him and preach to the people of Nineveh.**

Have children sit on the floor around the *Fold-Out Learning Mat: Jonah's Adventure*. Hold up the Bible. Say: **Our story today comes from the book of Jonah in the Bible.** Hold up the *Fold-Out Learning Mat*. Say: **Our Fold-Out Learning Mat shows us pictures of the story.** Unfold the *Fold-Out Mat* eight times to the picture of Jonah preaching to the people of Nineveh. Give each child a small cup of goldfish crackers. Say: **As we hear the next part of our story, listen carefully for the words "Nineveh" and "city." Each time you hear the words "Nineveh" or "city," you may eat a goldfish cracker.** Play the "Jonah's Adventure" segment (track 20) on the *CD*, unfolding the *Fold-Out Mat* when you hear the chime.

When the segment is finished, stop the *CD*. Say: **The Bible says Nineveh was so big that it took three whole days to walk around it. Let's be like Jonah and walk around the *Fold-Out Mat* three times. As we walk we'll chant, "Repent and turn to God."** Lead children in a walk around the *Fold-Out Mat* three times. Then ask them to sit down around the *Fold-Out Mat* again. Ask:

● **What did Jonah tell the people of Nineveh?** (God's angry at you; stop being bad; pray and be sorry.)

● **What did the people do when they heard Jonah?** (They prayed; they cried; they said they were sorry.)

● **Why did God forgive the people of Nineveh?** (He loved them; they were sorry; they asked him to.)

Say: **The people of Nineveh were sorry for what they had done. They prayed to God and asked for forgiveness. To show God how sorry they were, they put on scratchy clothes called sackcloth and they stopped eating. God saw they were truly sorry so he gave them another chance to obey.** Ask:

● **What do you do when you're sorry for something you've done?** (Pray; ask God to forgive me; tell God I'm sorry.)

Say: **God will give us another chance, just as he did for Jonah and the people of Nineveh. It's important to remember that ◐ God forgives us when we're sorry for what we've done. All the people in Nineveh were happy when God forgave them—all the people except one. Next week we'll find out who the unhappy person was. Right now I'm ready for a game.**

◐ **The Point**

Do the Bible Story (up to 10 minutes)

Have children form a line at one end of the room. Give the first child in line the paper *cape* from the Learning Lab. Place a few paper plates in a path leading to the opposite wall. Say: **The people of Nineveh wanted to show God that nothing mattered to them but his forgiveness. To show God how sorry they were, they skipped meals for a while so they could pray more, and they put on scratchy clothes called sackcloth. Let's pretend we're in Nineveh and this cape is sackcloth. The paper plates on the floor can stand for the meals that the people skipped. We'll hop around Nineveh, skipping the plates like the people skipped meals. As we go we'll say, "I won't eat or work or play, all I want to do is pray." Each time we hop around Nineveh, a different person will get to wear the *cape*. Ready? Let's go!** Demonstrate how to weave around the plates in a serpentine fashion.

When all the children have had a chance to wear the *cape*, say: **Today we've learned how 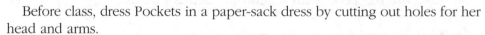 God forgives us when we're sorry for what we've done. When Jonah was sorry, God forgave him. And when the people of Nineveh were sorry, God forgave them, too. We need to remember that God forgives us when we're sorry for what we've done. Let's remember to tell Pockets how the people of Nineveh were sorry for what they had done.**

⬤ The Point

⬤ The Point

Practicing the Point

Sorry Sackcloth (up to 5 minutes)

Before class, dress Pockets in a paper-sack dress by cutting out holes for her head and arms.

Have children sit in a group. Take out Pockets the Kangaroo. Go through the following script. When you finish the script, put Pockets out of sight.

Sorry Sackcloth

PUPPET SCRIPT

Pockets: *(Comes in twirling her paper dress.)* Hi, everybody. Notice anything different? Hmmm?

Teacher: *(Raises eyebrows toward class.)* Well...Umm... You're dressed a little funny today.

Pockets: *(Twirling again)* What do you mean funny? Don't you like my new dress?

Teacher: Sure, Pockets, we like it. It's just that...well... you're wearing a paper bag.

Pockets: No, I'm not! It's a sack, just like the people in Nineveh wore. I heard you say they dressed in sacks!

(Continued)

God forgives us.

Teacher: Oh, I know what you're thinking. We were talking about how the people in Nineveh wanted to show God how sorry they were. Class, can you tell Pockets what the people in Nineveh did when they were sorry? *(Encourage children to tell Pockets how the people prayed, wore scratchy clothes, and stopped eating for a while.)*

Pockets: And did God forgive the people of Nineveh?

Teacher: Yes, Pockets. Just as he forgave Jonah. 🖊 God forgives us when we're sorry for what we've done.

Pockets: Hmmm. So they didn't wear paper sacks?

Teacher: No, I'm afraid not.

Pockets: Do I have to wear sackcloth when I'm sorry for something I've done?

Teacher: No. Class, what does she need to do to be forgiven? *(Encourage children to tell Pockets she needs to be really sorry, then pray and ask God for forgiveness.)*

Pockets: That's all? If I'm really and truly sorry, and I ask God to forgive me, he will?

Teacher: That's right, Pockets.

Pockets: *(Looking at her dress)* That's a relief! 'Cause this dress isn't very comfortable, you know. I think I'll go home now to change. 'Bye, everyone.
(Have children say goodbye.)

🖊 **The Point**

TODAY I LEARNED...

We believe that Christian education extends beyond the classroom into the home. Photocopy the "Today I Learned..." handout (p. 180) for this week and send it home with your children. Encourage parents to use the handout to plan meaningful family activities to reinforce this week's topic. Follow up the "Today I Learned..." activities next week by asking children what their families did.

Closing

Sorry From the Heart (up to 5 minutes)

Lead the children in singing "The Forgiveness Song" (track 21) with the *CD* to the tune of "Jesus Loves Me." For more fun, teach children the accompanying actions.

Sing

Silly Jonah ran away *(running motion)*,
But God still watched him day by day. *(Hand shading eyes.)*

God forgives us.

Jonah prayed inside a whale *(praying hands)*,
And God's forgiveness did not fail. *(Shake head no.)*

God will forgive us. *(Hands over heart.)*
God will forgive us.
God will forgive us
When we ask him to. *(Praying hands.)*

Like Jonah we may disobey *(shake forefinger)*,
But God forgives us when we pray. *(Praying hands.)*
Even if we try to hide *(arms in front of face)*,
God will still be on our side. *(Slap arms to sides.)*

God will forgive us. *(Hands over heart.)*
God will forgive us.
God will forgive us
When we ask him to. *(Praying hands.)*

● The Point

Say: **That sounded wonderful! I'm glad we've learned how ● God forgives us when we're sorry for what we've done. Let's thank God right now.** Pray: **Dear God, thank you for forgiving us when we're sorry for what we've done. In Jesus' name we pray, amen.**

God forgives us.

For Extra Time

If you have a long class time or want to add additional elements to your lesson, try one of the following activities.

LIVELY LEARNING: Pockets Says

Place the *Fold-Out Learning Mat: Jonah's Adventures* on the floor in the center of the room. Unfold the mat nine times to the picture of the people repenting in Nineveh. Bring out Pockets the Kangaroo. Say: **Instead of Simon Says, let's play Pockets Says. We'll use the *Fold-Out Learning Mat* to review our Bible story.** Have Pockets give the following directions. Allow time for children to respond between commands. Say:
- **Pockets says: Sit down near Joppa.**
- **Pockets says: Kneel by the boat and pretend to row.**
- **Pockets says: Pretend to swim around the mat.**
- **Pockets says: Touch the nose of the fish.**
- **Pockets says: Hop around the Mat and sit down at Nineveh.**

Discuss why it was important for the people of Nineveh to ask for forgiveness. Explain that they learned that God is loving because 🖊 God forgives us when we're sorry for what we've done.

🖊 The Point

MAKE TO TAKE: Forgiveness Necklaces

Before class, cut an 18-inch length of string for each child in your class. Set out the lengths of string, small pieces of burlap, and several staplers. Demonstrate how to tie the ends of a string together, then staple several pieces of burlap to the center of the string to make a necklace. Let each child make a necklace. Discuss how the people of Nineveh wore sackcloth to show God they wanted his forgiveness. Tell children they can wear their necklaces to remind them that 🖊 God forgives us when we're sorry for what we've done.

🖊 The Point

TREAT TO EAT: Sorry Sandwiches

Set out bread, peanut butter, marshmallow creme, and plastic knives.

Form three groups: the Better Butterers, the Crazy Creamers, and the Careful Cutters. Better Butterers will spread peanut butter on slices of bread. Crazy Creamers will spread marshmallow creme on top of the peanut butter. Careful Cutters will top each sandwich with another slice of bread, then cut into halves or quarters. As children enjoy their treats, talk about how the people of Nineveh wanted to show God how sorry they were. They were so busy praying they didn't even want to stop to eat! Remind children that God forgave the people of Nineveh because 🖊 God forgives us when we're sorry for what we've done.

🖊 The Point

STORY PICTURE: God Forgives the People of Nineveh

Give each child a photocopy of the "Today I Learned . . ." handout from page 180. Set out glue sticks and small scraps of burlap or other rough cloth. Let children glue the rough cloth on the robes of the people praying.

God forgives us.

TODAY I LEARNED...

The Point ✎ God forgives us when we're sorry for what we've done.

Today your child learned that God forgives us when we're sorry for what we've done. Children learned that it's important to feel sorry and to pray when they've done something wrong. They talked about how God will forgive them and give them another chance.

Verse to Learn

"You are forgiving and good, O Lord" (Psalm 86:5a).

Ask Me...

● How did the people of Nineveh show God they were sorry?

● What do you do to show you're sorry for something you've done?

● Why is it important for us to forgive people when they tell us they're sorry?

Family Fun

● Plan a special meal one day and call it a "Forgiveness Feast." Let children help prepare the food. Include on the menu Forgiveness Fish Sticks, Sackcloth Salad, and Tapioca Teardrop Pudding. Encourage your child to tell you the story of Jonah during the meal. Discuss how God forgave Jonah and the Ninevites when they were sorry for what they had done.

Jonah Preaches to the Ninevites (Jonah 3:1-10)

Love and Forgive-ness

LESSON 13

The Bible Basis

Jonah 4:1-11. God forgives the people of Nineveh.

When the people of Nineveh sincerely repented, God mercifully forgave them. Jonah's negative attitude about the Ninevites quickly kindled into anger. He sat sulking east of the city, his prayers full of frustration. God saw the situation and arranged a subtle sign to nudge Jonah toward compassion. He caused a shady vine to grow over Jonah, then sent a worm to destroy that comfort from the hot sun. When Jonah cried out to God, God brought his point home. How could Jonah care so much about a vine he had no hand in making? How could he expect God not to care about people he had created? Jonah willingly accepted God's forgiveness for himself but disdained the thought of mercy for Nineveh. Jonah finally had to accept God's sovereignty and realize that God offers love and forgiveness to all people.

"It's not fair!" is a hallmark phrase of childhood. It's not fair when the neighbor gets a new bike, even though he's a bully on the playground. It's not fair that Mary's sister gets an allowance when she doesn't do as many chores as Mary. It's not fair that the teacher gives Bobby extra stickers on his paper. To adults, these complaints seem trivial. But how did Jonah's complaints sound to God? (Or our complaints, for that matter?) God can see the big picture—he knows what's hidden in every heart. Help children understand that God's forgiveness is so great because his love is so great and that God knows what is fair better than we do.

Getting the Point

✎ **God forgives us because he loves us.**

It's important to say The Point just as it's written in each activity. Repeating The Point over and over will help the children remember it and apply it to their lives.

Children will

● learn that God forgives us because he loves us,

● understand that God loved Jonah even when Jonah was angry,

● help Pockets understand how much God loves us, and

● see that God keeps loving and forgiving us, even when we're angry.

✎ **The Point**

This Lesson at a Glance

Before the lesson, collect the necessary items for the activities you plan to use. Refer to the Classroom Supplies and Learning Lab Supplies columns to determine what you'll need. Remember to make photocopies of the "Today I Learned..." handout (p. 192) to send home with your children.

Section	Minutes	What Children Will Do	Classroom Supplies	Learning Lab Supplies
Welcome Time	up to 5	**Welcome!**—Receive name tags and be greeted by the teacher.	"Family Name Tags" handouts (p. 29), markers, pins or tape	
Let's Get Started Direct children to one or more of the Let's Get Started activities until everyone arrives.	up to 10	**Option 1: Clay Capers**—Make clay figures to review the story of Jonah in the Bible.	Modeling dough, vinyl place mats	
	up to 10	**Option 2: Jonah Puppets**—Make Jonah puppets to use later in the lesson.	Craft sticks, glue, scissors, crayons, markers, "Jonah" handout (p. 154)	
	up to 10	**Option 3: Tumbling Tumblers**—Learn about forgiveness while playing a fun paper-cup game.	Paper cups, masking tape, markers	Pretend rock
Pick-Up Song	up to 5	**We Will Pick Up**—Sing a song as they pick up toys and gather for Bible-Story Time.	CD player	CD: "We Will Pick Up" (track 2)
Bible-Story Time	up to 5	**Setting the Stage**—Flip a coin and learn that only God knows how things will work out.	Pennies	
	up to 5	**Bible Song and Prayer Time**—Sing a song, bring out the Bible, and pray together.	Bible, construction paper, scissors, basket or box, CD player	CD: "God's Book" (track 3), great fish stamp and ink pad
	up to 10	**Hear the Bible Story**—Use their Jonah puppets to help tell the story of Jonah from Jonah 4:1-11.	Bible, Jonah puppets from Option 2, CD player	Fold-Out Learning Mat: Jonah's Adventure, CD: "Jonah's Adventure" (track 22)
	up to 10	**Do the Bible Story**—Play a fun game of musical fish and actively review the story of Jonah.	"Big Fish" handout (p. 167), tape, CD player, fish-shaped crackers	CD: "The Forgiveness Song" (track 21)
Practicing the Point	up to 5	**Fishing for Forgiveness**—Help teach Pockets about God's love and forgiveness.	Pockets the Kangaroo, stick-and-string fishing rod, gummy worms	
Closing	up to 5	**Happy Hearts**—Decorate edible hearts, then pray.	Cookies, icing, sprinkles, plastic knives	
For Extra Time		For extra-time ideas and supplies, see page 191.		

God forgives us.

Welcome Time

Welcome! (up to 5 minutes)

- Bend down to make eye contact with children as they arrive.
- Greet each child individually with an enthusiastic smile.
- Thank each child for coming to class today.
- As children arrive, ask them about last week's "Today I Learned..." discussion. Ask questions such as "What did Jonah tell the people of Nineveh?" and "How were you forgiven last week or who did you forgive?"
- Say: **Today we're going to learn that** ◗ **God forgives us because he loves us.**

◗ **The Point**

- Hand out the "Family" name tags children made in Lesson 1 and help them attach the name tags to their clothing. If some of the name tags were damaged or if some of the children weren't in class that week, have them make new name tags using the photocopiable handout on page 29.
- Direct the children to the Let's Get Started activities you've set up.

Let's Get Started

Set up one or more of the following activities for children to do as they arrive. After you greet each child, invite him or her to choose an activity.

Circulate among the children to offer help as needed and direct children's conversation toward today's lesson. Ask questions such as "What kinds of things make you mad?" or "How do you feel when someone forgives you?"

☐ OPTION 1: Clay Capers (up to 10 minutes)

Set modeling dough and vinyl place mats on a table. Invite children to make shapes and characters found in the story of Jonah. Suggest that children make fish, boats, and Jonah figures. As children work, ask them to mention things in the story that made Jonah angry or afraid. Explain that today children will learn about a time Jonah was mad at God and how God forgave him. Tell children that ◗ God forgives us because he loves us.

◗ **The Point**

☐ OPTION 2: Jonah Puppets (up to 10 minutes)

Before class, photocopy the "Jonah" handout from page 154. You'll need one copy for each child in your class. Set out craft sticks, glue, the Jonah patterns, scissors, crayons, and markers. Invite children to make Jonah puppets by coloring and cutting out the Jonah figures, then gluing them to the craft sticks. As children work, ask questions such as "Have you ever forgiven someone or been forgiven?" Tell children that today they'll hear how God forgave Jonah. Explain that ◗ God forgives us because he loves us.

◗ **The Point**

God forgives us.

☐ OPTION 3: Tumbling Tumblers (up to 10 minutes)

Set out paper cups, masking tape, markers, and the *pretend rock* from the Learning Lab box. Tape a starting line on the floor. Give each child a paper cup. Have children write their names on their cups, then set them on the floor about three feet in front of the starting line. Have children form a line behind the starting line. Each child will take a turn tossing the *pretend rock*, trying to knock over as many cups as possible with one toss. After taking a turn, each child will move behind the cups and help set them up for the next child. As children work together setting up the cups, make comments such as "I'm happy that you're able to forgive each other when your cups are knocked over" and "Today we'll hear how Jonah learned that ● God forgives us because he loves us."

● The Point

When everyone has arrived and you're ready to move on to the Bible-Story Time, encourage the children to finish what they're doing and get ready to clean up.

Pick-Up Song

We Will Pick Up (up to 5 minutes)

Lead children in singing "We Will Pick Up" (track 2) with the *CD* to the tune of "London Bridge." Encourage the children to sing along as they help clean up the room.

If you want to include the names of all the children in your class, sing "We Will Pick Up" without the *CD*. If you choose to use the *CD*, vary the names you use each week.

Sing

We will pick up all our toys,
All our toys, all our toys.
We will pick up all our toys
And put them all away.

I see (name) picking up,
Picking up, picking up.
I see (name) picking up
And putting toys away.

(Repeat.)

God forgives us.

Bible-Story Time

Setting the Stage (up to 5 minutes)

Tell the children you'll clap your hands to get their attention. Explain that when you clap your hands, children are to stop what they're doing, raise their hands, and focus on you. Encourage children to respond quickly so you'll have time for all the fun activities you've planned.

Before this activity, gather enough pennies so every pair of children in your class will have one. Have children sit together in a circle on the floor. Say: **Let's have a coin toss! We'll form pairs, and I'll give each pair a coin.** Hold up a penny. Say: **The side of the coin with the picture of a person's head is called "heads." The other side is called "tails."** Have children find partners and give each pair a penny. Let partners decide who will be the Flipper and who will be the Guesser. Explain that the Guesser will predict whether the flipped coin will be heads or tails. Then have the Flipper toss the coin and see which side the coin lands on. After three guesses and flips, have partners switch roles. Then ask:

● **Were you able to guess how the coin would land every time?** (No; we were wrong some of the time; we couldn't tell what would happen.)

● **How did guessing wrong make you feel?** (Silly; mad; upset.)

● **Do you think it's possible to tell what God's plans are? Why or why not?** (No; we can't tell what God will do; only God knows his plans.)

Say: **Just like we couldn't always tell what the coin would do, we can't always tell what God's plans are. When God doesn't do what we think he should, we may get angry with God. That's what happened to Jonah. Jonah didn't think God should forgive the people of Nineveh. But God did forgive them. Today we're learning that ⬛ God forgives us because he loves us. Now let's get ready for our Bible story.**

Collect the pennies and set them aside.

⬤ The Point

Bible Song and Prayer Time (up to 5 minutes)

Before class, make surprise cards for this activity by cutting construction paper in 2×6-inch slips. Prepare a surprise card for each child plus a few extras for visitors. Fold the cards in half, then stamp the *great fish stamp* inside one of the surprise cards. Mark Jonah 4:1-11 in the Bible you'll be using.

Have the children sit in a circle. Say: **Now it's time to choose a Bible person to bring me the Bible marked with today's Bible story. As we sing our Bible song, I'll pass out the surprise cards. Don't look inside your card until the song is over.**

Lead children in singing "God's Book" (track 3) with the *CD* to the tune of "Old MacDonald Had a Farm." As you sing, pass out the surprise cards. If you want to include the names of all the children in your class, sing "God's Book" without the *CD*. If you choose to use the *CD*, vary the names you use each week.

Sing

Now it's time to read God's Book
And hear a Bible story.
It's fun to be here with my
  friends
And hear a Bible story.
	Now it's time to read God's Book
	And hear a Bible story.
	It's fun to be here with my
	  friends
	And hear a Bible story.

(Name)'s here. (Name)'s here. Here is (name). Here is (name). Now it's time to read God's Book And hear a Bible story.	(Name)'s here. (Name)'s here. Here is (name). Here is (name). Now it's time to read God's Book And hear a Bible story.

After the song, say: **You may look inside your surprise cards. The person who has the great fish stamped inside his or her card will be our Bible person for today.**

Identify the Bible person, then have the rest of the children clap for him or her. Ask the Bible person to bring you the Bible. Help the Bible person open the Bible to the marked place and show the children where your story comes from. Then have the Bible person sit down.

Say: (Name) **was our special Bible person today. Each week, we'll have only one Bible person, but each of you is a special part of our class! Today we're all learning that ✎ God forgives us because he loves us.**

✎ The Point

Let's say a special prayer now and ask God to help us learn more about his love. I'll pass around this basket. When the basket comes to you, put your surprise card in it and say, "God, help us learn more about your forgiving love."

Pass around the basket or box. When you've collected everyone's surprise card, set the basket aside and pick up the Bible. Lead children in this prayer: **God, thank you for the Bible and all the stories in it. Teach us today that ✎ you forgive us because you love us. In Jesus' name we pray, amen.**

✎ The Point

Hear the Bible Story (up to 10 minutes)

Have children sit in a circle on the floor around the closed *Fold-Out Learning Mat: Jonah's Adventure*. Say: **Last week we heard how Jonah preached to the people of Nineveh. Let's open our *Fold-Out Learning Mat* and review the story as we look at the pictures.** Have children form pairs. Have pairs take turns unfolding the mat, retelling the story in their own words. Unfold the *Fold-Out Learning Mat* until you reveal the picture of Jonah sitting under the vine.

Say: **All the people in Nineveh were happy when God forgave them. All the people except one!** Ask:

● **Who do you suppose was unhappy because God forgave the people of Nineveh?** (Jonah; I don't know.)

Say: **Jonah was unhappy. In fact, he was really mad! He didn't like the people of Nineveh and didn't think God should forgive them. So he left the city and sat down to pout. God made a shady vine grow quickly above Jonah to protect him from the hot sun.** Give each child a Jonah puppet made in Option 2. **Let's listen to the rest of our story, and find out how God taught Jonah about forgiveness. I'll need your help to tell the story. Every time you hear the name "Jonah," hold your Jonah puppets in the air as high as you can. When you hear the word "worm," wiggle your pointer fingers. And when you hear the word "forgive," put your hands over your hearts.**

Play the "Jonah's Adventure" segment (track 22) on the *CD*, unfolding the *Fold-Out Learning Mat* when you hear the chime. When the segment ends, turn off the CD player.

Ask:

● **Why was Jonah mad at God?** (Because God forgave the people of Nineveh; because God sent the worm; because God took away his shade.)

● **Why did God send the worm to take away Jonah's shade?** (To show Jonah that God is in charge of everything; to make Jonah sorry for being mad; to teach Jonah a lesson.)

● **Have you ever been angry when something good happened to someone else? Why or why not?** (Let children respond.)

Say: **Sometimes we feel angry and jealous like Jonah. It's easy to feel like Jonah did, sometimes. We want to keep God's love and forgiveness for ourselves and may think others don't deserve those good things. It's important to remember that God loves everyone and wants to forgive them if they're sorry.** Ask:

● **Why did God forgive Jonah?** (Because Jonah was sorry; because God is good; because God loved Jonah.)

● **Why did God forgive the people of Nineveh?** (Because they were sorry; because they prayed; because God loved them.)

Say: **We can use the story of Jonah to remind us that 🖊 God forgives us because he loves us. Let's play a fun game to help us remember the story of Jonah and of how God used a big fish and a little worm to teach Jonah about his love.**

Do the Bible Story (up to 10 minutes)

Before class, photocopy the "Big Fish" handout from page 167. Make one copy of the fish handout for every child in your class. On a separate sheet of paper, draw a worm with a smiley face. Tape the fish and worm papers in a circle on the floor and place a plate of fish-shaped crackers in the center of the circle.

Say: **Let's play a musical game to review the story of Jonah. I'll play "The Forgiveness Song." As the music plays, hop from picture to picture around the circle. When the music stops, whoever is standing on the worm will get to answer a Jonah question. After you've answered, you may "swim" to the center of the circle for a fishy treat.**

Start "The Forgiveness Song" (track 21) on the *CD* and have children hop around the circle. Pause the song at intervals. During each interval, ask whoever is standing on the worm one of the following questions. Make sure each child gets a chance to answer a question and swim for a treat. Ask:

● **What did God tell Jonah to do in the beginning of the story?** (Go to Nineveh; obey; preach to the people.)

● **What did Jonah do instead of obeying God?** (He ran away; he tried to hide; he jumped on a boat.)

🖊 **The Point**

- **How did Jonah end up in the sea?** (The sailors threw him overboard; he was thrown in during a storm.)
- **Why didn't Jonah drown when he was thrown into the water?** (God sent a big fish to swallow Jonah; a fish saved him from drowning.)
- **What did Jonah do inside the big fish?** (He prayed to God; he told God he was sorry; he asked God to let him out.)
- **When Jonah prayed, what did God tell the fish to do?** (Spit Jonah out; take Jonah to dry land.)
- **What did Jonah tell the people of Nineveh?** (Stop being bad; pray to God; ask for forgiveness.)
- **Why did God forgive Jonah and the people of Nineveh?** (He loved them; they were sorry; they prayed.)

Say: **Everyone did a great job remembering! Let's all clap for each other.** (Let children respond.) **We've learned a lot from Jonah, haven't we? We've learned that God forgives us even when we disobey and cause trouble. But when we're sorry for what we've done and pray to God, he forgives us.** Ask:

 **The Point**

- **Why does God forgive us?** (Because he loves us.)

Say: **That's right.** 🖊 **God forgives us because he loves us. And to think it took a wiggly worm to help Jonah learn about God's forgiveness. Pockets was looking for a worm earlier. Let's see why Pockets wants a worm.**

Practicing the Point

Fishing for Forgiveness (up to 5 minutes)

Before class, put a simple fishing rod and a bag of gummy worms in Pockets' pouch. You can make the rod by tying a string to a stick. Have children sit in a circle. Take out Pockets the Kangaroo. Go through the following script. When you finish the script, put Pockets out of sight.

Fishing For Forgiveness
PUPPET SCRIPT

Pockets: *(With fishing rod in her pocket)* Hi, everybody. Are you ready?

Teacher: Hello, Pockets. Ready for what?

Pockets: Ready for what? For fishing, of course. I brought my fishing rod. *(Holds the fishing rod.)* Where are the worms?

Teacher: Pockets, we're not going fishing today. And we don't have any worms.

Pockets: But I heard you say something about a worm. So I ran right home to get my fishing rod. I love worms! They're so wiggly and wriggly. And slimy, too!

(Continued)

God forgives us.

Teacher: Well, there <u>was</u> a worm in our Bible story today. We heard how Jonah was mad at God because he forgave the people of Nineveh. So he left the city and sat under a shady vine to pout. Then God sent a worm to visit Jonah. Class, can you tell Pockets about the worm God sent to eat Jonah's vine? *(Encourage children to explain how Jonah was angry because God forgave the Ninevites, and how he sent a worm to destroy the vine.)*

Pockets: Wow! That must have been some worm. I guess Jonah was pretty upset when the worm ate his vine. That probably made him even madder.

Teacher: Yes, it did—at first. But God sent the worm to teach Jonah a very important lesson about forgiveness.

Pockets: What lesson?

Teacher: That  God forgives us because he loves us. Jonah cared about a vine he didn't make. Just imagine how much more God cares about the people he makes.

Pockets: Oh, I see. Jonah was upset about some old vine he didn't even make. But God made us, and he loves us, too. Right?

Teacher: Right, Pockets. And because God loves us, he wants to forgive us when we do something wrong.

Pockets: I'm glad. We all need forgiveness sometimes—just like Jonah. I'm sure glad God loves us.

Teacher: We're glad, too. Aren't we, class? *(Let children respond.)*

Pockets: I learned a lot today. Thanks for teaching me about forgiveness—and worms! Hey, that reminds me. When I found some worms earlier, I decided to bring you some, too. *(Have Pockets take the bag of gummy worms from her pouch and share them with the children.)* Well, I think I'll go fishing now. 'Bye, everyone.

(Have children say goodbye.)

● **The Point**

TODAY I LEARNED . . .

We believe that Christian education extends beyond the classroom into the home. Photocopy the "Today I Learned . . ." handout (p. 192) for this week and send it home with your children. Encourage parents to use the handout to plan meaningful family activities to reinforce this week's topic. Follow up the "Today I Learned . . ." activities next week by asking children what their families did.

Closing

Happy Hearts (up to 5 minutes)

● The Point

Purchase heart-shaped sugar cookies from the store or bake heart-shaped cookies for your class. Set out cookies, icing, sprinkles, and plastic knives. Let children decorate the cookies with icing and sprinkles. Remind children how happy the people of Nineveh were when God forgave them and that our hearts are happy that ●God forgives us because he loves us. As you enjoy eating your special treats, encourage children to tell about a time they were forgiven and how they felt.

Say: **Before we go, let's say a short prayer to thank God for his love and forgiveness.** Pray: **Dear God, thank you for forgiving us and loving us, too. In Jesus' name we pray, amen.**

If you have time before the end of class, sing "The Forgiveness Song," without the *CD,* to the tune of "Jesus Loves Me."

> Silly Jonah ran away,
> But God still watched him day by day.
> Jonah prayed inside a whale,
> And God's forgiveness did not fail.
>
> God will forgive us.
> God will forgive us.
> God will forgive us,
> When we ask him to.
>
> Like Jonah we may disobey,
> But God forgives us when we pray.
> Even if we try to hide,
> God will still be on our side.
>
> God will forgive us.
> God will forgive us.
> God will forgive us,
> When we ask him to.

For Extra Time

If you have a long class time or want to add additional elements to your lesson, try one of the following activities.

LIVELY LEARNING: Listening Center

Let children listen to the entire story of "Jonah's Adventure" (track 23) on the *CD*. Set out the *Fold-Out Learning Mat: Jonah's Adventure* and the CD player in a corner of the room. Choose one child to unfold the *Fold-Out Learning Mat*. Assure children that they'll each have a turn to be a helper another time. (You may wish to keep a record of the children who have been helpers.) Be sure to tell children to listen for the sound of the chime and unfold the *Learning Mat* when they hear it. The entire recorded version of "Jonah's Adventure" is track 23 on the *CD*.

MAKE TO TAKE: Worm Paintings

Before class, cook enough strands of spaghetti so every child in your class will have one. Cover your work area with newsprint. Set out white paper, several small bowls of paints, and cooked spaghetti. Let each child make a "worm painting" by dipping a spaghetti noodle into the paint and wriggling it around on a sheet of paper. When everyone has made a painting, discard the spaghetti. Talk about how God sent the worm to teach Jonah that he loves all people and wants to forgive them. Tell children it's important to remember that ✏ God forgives us because he loves us.

● The Point

TREAT TO EAT: Wormy Wonders

Let children make garden treats—complete with worms! Set out lettuce, a few spoons, small paper plates, a large empty bowl, and a bowl of gummy worms. Form three groups: the Lettuce Shredders, the Plate Passers, and the Worm Diggers. The Lettuce Shredders will rip the lettuce into small pieces and place the pieces in the empty bowl. Plate Passers will put some shredded lettuce on each plate and pass the plates on to the Worm Diggers. Worm Diggers will use spoons to dig the worms out of the bowl and place one worm (or more) on each plate. (For extra fun, put the worms in a bowl of "dirt," actually powdered chocolate drink mix.) Discuss how God used the worm to teach Jonah that God's love and forgiveness are offered to everyone. Remind children that ✏ God forgives us because he loves us.

● The Point

STORY PICTURE: Pouting Jonah

Give each child a photocopy of the "Today I Learned..." handout from page 192. Set out crayons, glue, and artificial leaves. Let children color their pictures and glue artificial leaves onto their vines. As children work, ask them to recount the story of Jonah.

TODAY I LEARNED...

The Point ● God forgives us because he loves us.

LESSON 13

Today your child learned that God forgives us because he loves us. Children learned that even though Jonah disapproved, God's love and forgiveness extended to the Ninevites, too. Children talked about being more forgiving themselves.

Verse to Learn

"You are forgiving and good, O Lord" (Psalm 86:5a).

Ask Me...

● Why was Jonah mad at God?
● Have you ever been mad at someone you love?
● What should we do at home when we're angry?

Family Fun

● Write a Family Love Letter. Have the family sit down at a table together. Write each family member's name on a sheet of paper. Under each name, list qualities or actions the family appreciates about that person. Go around the table and give each person a chance to share their comments. The discussion might include statements such as "Dad helps me play baseball" or "Mom always reads to me." Hang the love letter in a prominent place during the coming week.

God Forgives the People of Nineveh (Jonah 4:1-11)